The Role of Districts in Fostering Instructional Improvement

Lessons from Three Urban Districts Partnered with the Institute for Learning

Julie A. Marsh, Kerri A. Kerr, Gina S. Ikemoto, Hilary Darilek,
Marika Suttorp, Ron W. Zimmer, Heather Barney

Supported by The William and Flora Hewlett Foundation

 EDUCATION

The research described in this report was conducted within RAND Education and supported by The William and Flora Hewlett Foundation.

Library of Congress Cataloging-in-Publication Data

The role of districts in fostering instructional improvement : lessons from three urban districts partnered with the Institute for Learning / Julie A. Marsh ... [et al.].
    p. cm.
    "MG-361."
    Includes bibliographical references.
    ISBN 0-8330-3853-2 (pbk. : alk. paper)
    1. School improvement programs—United States—Case studies. 2. Instructional systems—United States—Case studies. 3. School districts—United States—Case studies. 4. Educational change—United States—Case studies. I. Marsh, Julie A. II. Institute for Learning.

LB2822.82.R64 2005
379.1'5350973—dc22

                                                              2005025509

Cover photo: Media Bakery at www.mediabakery.com

The RAND Corporation is a nonprofit research organization providing objective analysis and effective solutions that address the challenges facing the public and private sectors around the world. RAND's publications do not necessarily reflect the opinions of its research clients and sponsors.

RAND® is a registered trademark.

Published 2005 by the RAND Corporation
1776 Main Street, P.O. Box 2138, Santa Monica, CA 90407-2138
1200 South Hayes Street, Arlington, VA 22202-5050
201 North Craig Street, Suite 202, Pittsburgh, PA 15213-1516
RAND URL: http://www.rand.org/
To order RAND documents or to obtain additional information, contact
Distribution Services: Telephone: (310) 451-7002;
Fax: (310) 451-6915; Email: order@rand.org

Preface

The current high-stakes accountability environment brought on by the federal No Child Left Behind Act (NCLB) places great pressure on school districts to demonstrate success by meeting yearly progress goals for student achievement and eventually demonstrating that all students achieve at high standards. In particular, many urban school districts—with their high-poverty and low-achieving student population and constraints due to insufficient human, physical, and financial resources and high rates of turnover in school and district staff—face great challenges in meeting these goals.

In fall 2002, the RAND Corporation initiated a study to analyze three urban districts' efforts to face these challenges and improve the instructional quality and performance of their schools. The study also sought to assess the contribution to these efforts made by an intermediary organization, the Institute for Learning (IFL). We closely examined district reform efforts in four areas: promoting the instructional leadership of principals; supporting the professional learning of teachers, in particular through school-based coaching models; specifying curriculum; and promoting data-based decision-making for planning and instructional improvement. We also examined the impact of the IFL on these instructional improvement efforts.

This monograph presents findings from that three-year study. It describes the districts' work in each area of reform, identifies common constraints and enablers of district success, assesses the nature and impact of district-intermediary partnerships, and makes recommendations for districts undertaking similar instructional reforms.

The report should interest policymakers, researchers, and practitioners involved in designing, implementing, assisting, or studying school districts' efforts to improve the instructional quality and performance of all schools.

This research was undertaken within RAND Education, a unit of the RAND Corporation. Funding to carry out the work was provided by The William and Flora Hewlett Foundation.

Dedication

We dedicate this report to the memory of RAND's Tom Glennan, a dear colleague, friend, and mentor to all of us involved in this study. Tom initiated this research out of a profound commitment to better understanding and supporting the work of urban school districts.

Contents

CHAPTER FIVE

Figures

Tables

Summary

Improving school systems is critical to bridging the achievement gap between students of different racial and socioeconomic backgrounds and to achieving the goals of the No Child Left Behind Act (NCLB). In fall 2002, the RAND Corporation initiated a formative assessment of three urban districts' efforts to improve instructional quality and school performance. The study explored ways to improve teaching and learning in urban school districts. It also examined the contributions of one intermediary organization, the Institute for Learning (IFL), to efforts to introduce systemic change in the three districts. The study sought to answer four broad questions:

- What strategies did districts employ to promote instructional improvement? How did these strategies work?
- What were the constraints and enablers of district instructional improvement efforts?
- What was the impact of the IFL? What were the constraints and enablers of the district-IFL partnerships?
- What are the implications for district instructional improvement and district-intermediary partnerships?

Methods

We used a comparative case study design and mixed methods to answer these questions. Districts were selected for experience working with the IFL (more than three years) and for variation in district size, union environment, and state context. We collected and analyzed data from extensive field interviews and focus groups conducted over a two-year period; from RAND-developed surveys of elementary, middle, and high school principals and teachers; from district and IFL documents; and from demographic and student achievement databases.

Findings

Our evidence yielded the following findings.

District Instructional Improvement Strategies

In the three districts, instructional reform efforts revolved around four common areas of focus: building the instructional leadership skills of principals; supporting the professional learning of teachers, with a particular focus on school-based coaching; providing greater specification of and support for standards-aligned curriculum; and promoting the use of data to guide instructional decisions. While all districts pursued strategies within each area, each tended to focus on two key areas to change the system. In addition, districts had varying degrees of success in attaining the intermediate reform goals (i.e., outcomes expected to ultimately contribute to improved teaching and learning). Our findings in the four areas of reform are as follows.

Instructional Leadership. All districts attempted to increase principals' instructional leadership capacity, giving principals professional development and expecting principals' supervisors (who typically had titles such as area or assistant superintendent) to focus school visits and meetings with principals on matters related to improving instruction.

Despite a relatively consistent focus on instructional leadership, principals varied greatly in the extent to which they acted as instructional leaders. While our data do not definitively explain this variation, several factors enabled district efforts: high-quality professional development and supportive supervisors who helped principals develop instructional leadership skills and implement them daily. Other factors limited this ability: lack of time and lack of credibility—that is, teachers did not view their principals as knowledgeable about instruction.

School-Based Coaching. Two districts invested in school-based instructional coaches as a means of providing ongoing, job-embedded professional development for teachers, but each implemented a different model. Although both models were intended to build the instructional capacity of schools and support district initiatives, *teachers tended to prefer the more flexible, school-centered approach to coaching rather than the relatively standardized curriculum-centered one.* The perceived value and effectiveness of coaches by teachers was greater when (1) coaches tailored their work to school and teacher needs, (2) coaches advised teachers about instruction, (3) time was available to meet with teachers, and (4) roles were clearly defined.

Curriculum Specification. All districts developed and implemented curriculum guidance documents that were intended to improve alignment of instruction with state standards and assessments and to increase consistency of instruction across classrooms and schools by specifying districtwide guidelines for the scope, pacing, and content of curriculum. Two districts invested significant resources into developing and monitoring teachers' use of the documents.

While district and school staff generally viewed the curriculum guides as useful for planning, promoting consistency of instruction, and helping principals observe and monitor teachers, teachers reported a limited effect on pedagogy. That is, teachers reported that guides influenced "when" and "what" they taught, but they did not make major shifts in "how" they taught the curriculum. Teachers were apt to value and use the guides when they perceived them to be aligned with state tests, received them in a timely manner, and participated in the development process. However, many teachers in all districts described the pacing and content of the guides as conflicting with their need to tailor instruction to individual students.

Data Use. The study districts invested to varying degrees in multiple strategies promoting the use of data to guide instructional decisions, such as providing professional development on how to interpret test results and encouraging structured reviews of student work. However, two districts focused much more on use of data. One emphasized the school improvement planning (SIP) process. The second district focused on interim assessments, designed to provide an "early warning system on progress being made" toward meeting state standards.

Teachers and principals in both districts generally found the various sources of data useful and reported using them regularly to identify areas of weakness and to guide instructional decisions. Principals and teachers in the district that focused on the SIP process, however, described the process as overly labor-intensive. Furthermore, teachers in the district that focused on interim assessments were less enthusiastic about these assessments than principals, preferring more timely, regular classroom assessment data. The efforts of both districts to focus on data were enabled by long-standing state accountability systems, accessibility and timeliness of data, teachers' views of the assessment results as valid measures of students' knowledge and ability, and the degree to which school staff received training and support for analyzing and interpreting data.

Constraints and Enablers of Instructional Improvement

Once district leaders had designed their reform strategies and put them into place, a number of common factors affected districts' success in bringing about the intermediate outcomes they intended for each set of strategies. Taken as a whole, these factors led to several cross-cutting findings:

- **Although it was important for districts to implement comprehensive reform, they benefited from focusing on a small number of initiatives.** While seemingly counter-intuitive, the combination of comprehensiveness—a systemic approach, strategies addressing all dimensions of instruction, and a dual focus on infrastructure and direct support—and focus on two key areas of reform proved to be important for instructional reform in all three districts.

- **District and school capacity greatly affected reform efforts.** While focusing on a few priority initiatives may have helped conserve limited resources to some extent, all districts nonetheless faced significant capacity gaps that hindered instructional improvement. According to district and school staff across the sites, capacity gaps that were most detrimental were *insufficient time* (e.g., for planning, to act as instructional leaders), *lack and/or instability of fiscal or physical resources* (e.g., instructional materials, funding), and *limited capacity of central office staff* (e.g., inadequate numbers, lack of expertise).
- **The broader policy context created both enabling and constraining conditions for district reform.** For example, some union policies hindered reform in two districts, and state and federal accountability policies shaped much of the districts' work with curriculum and data use.
- **Districts' success also was tied to several key dimensions and characteristics of the policies they developed.** District progress at achieving intermediate instructional improvement goals hinged in large part on the degree to which strategies
  —were aligned and mutually supportive
  —enabled multiple stakeholders to engage in reform
  —balanced standardization and flexibility
  —used local accountability policies to provide incentives for meaningful change.

Overall, districts generally struggled to achieve these policy features, which might be better characterized as common challenges or tensions that districts faced in achieving systemwide change.

Effect of IFL on District Instructional Reform

Partnerships with the IFL contributed to district reform in all three districts. In exchange for a fee, the IFL provided districts with a variety of resources, including on-site technical assistance from IFL resident fellows, opportunities to attend national meetings with other partner districts, advice from IFL leaders, and access to research, materials, and other tools. The IFL did not present an intervention or model for districts to implement as such but instead acted as a "coach," assisting districts with various aspects of instructional improvement appropriate to each local context.

In examining the IFL role in supporting district work in the four areas of instructional reform, we found that the strongest reported contributions of IFL were to systemwide efforts to build the instructional leadership of administrators. At all three sites, the IFL influenced the design and implementation of professional development opportunities for principals and central office staff, frequently delivering monthly training sessions and providing supporting materials that elucidated what it meant to be an instructional leader. According to district and IFL leaders, the IFL's contribution to other areas of reform—data use, coaching, and curriculum specification—was not as strong or as consistent across sites.

Overall, two findings emerged from our analysis of the IFL contributions to district reform.

1. **District and school leaders reported that the IFL affected the organizational culture, norms, and beliefs about instruction.** District leaders reported shifts in beliefs and norms around a set of ideas emphasized in IFL materials, professional development, and technical assistance. These included effort-based intelligence, two-way accountability, a focus on instruction and learning, the idea that everyone is a learner, and instruction as a public endeavor.
2. **The IFL was credited with helping develop the knowledge and skills of central office and school administrators.** The majority of principals in all three districts reported that professional development opportunities organized by the IFL and the districts improved their skills as instructional leaders, deepened their

knowledge about learning, and provided them with a common language facilitating dialogue. Similarly, central office leaders and staff reported that IFL staff pushed them to focus on instruction and system-level structures and policies that enabled high-quality instruction. They also reported that the IFL helped them become more knowledgeable about instruction and more skilled at supervising and supporting principals.

Both of these reported effects address key challenges facing districts undertaking systemic reform—namely, a lack of alignment among district initiatives and limited capacity to undertake reform. By providing a common set of ideas concerning teaching and learning, the IFL may have helped districts build mutually supportive reform strategies around a common vision of high-quality instruction. By enhancing principals' and central office administrators' knowledge and skills, the IFL also may have helped build the overall capacity of the district to lead instructional change across a system of schools.

Finally, several common factors appeared to influence IFL partnerships with the districts and its impact on them. The effect of the IFL was particularly strong when

- district and school leaders (e.g., superintendent, mid-level managers, principals) bought into the IFL's work
- IFL staff were viewed as trustworthy, credible, and having expertise that matched a particular district need
- the IFL offered practical tools to support implementation of theoretical ideas.

In some cases, however, the IFL's influence was constrained by

- the perception of IFL as a vendor brought in to provide particular services without much coordination and support from district leaders
- the IFL's limited capacity to support districts in all areas of reform
- turnover within the districts and the IFL.

Lessons Learned

The experiences of these three urban districts and their partnerships with the IFL provide evidence of promising results from systemwide instructional improvement efforts, yet they also raise warnings for districts and intermediary organizations about several important challenges they might face when attempting similar reforms. Our case studies also show that an intermediary organization can help districts address persistent constraints on reform by building the capacity of district staff to engage in instructional change and by facilitating policy alignment.

Lessons for Instructional Improvement

Based on the reform experiences of the three study districts, we offer the following lessons learned:

- Investing in the professional development of central office staff can enhance capacity to lead instructional reform.
- Instituting local accountability policies that create incentives for meaningful change can promote implementation.
- Aligning and developing a comprehensive set of strategies can reinforce overarching instructional improvement goals.

Lessons for District-Intermediary Partnerships

Although the specific characteristics of the IFL set it apart from some other types of third-party organizations, its experiences in these three districts nevertheless offer potentially useful insights for similar organizations as well as for districts considering similar partnerships. We present the following observations:

- Buy-in and support from top-level leaders can affect partnership viability.
- Preexisting reform initiatives and partnerships are important to consider when forming new partnerships.

- The capacity of the intermediary organization and its alignment with district needs can greatly affect partnership success.
- Practical tools that are perceived to be relevant and legitimate to the district's local context are needed.
- Multiple types of "scale-up" strategies can be relevant to system-wide change efforts.
- Defining and measuring partnership goals and progress may facilitate improvements and help sustain partnerships over time.

In the end, the experiences of these three urban districts and their partnerships with the IFL provide encouraging results regarding the role that districts and intermediary organizations can play in improving instruction, and valuable lessons about factors that constrain and enable the implementation and impact of such efforts.

Acknowledgments

Many individuals contributed to this report. First, we are grateful to leaders in the three study districts and the Institute for Learning for allowing us to conduct this research. We deeply appreciate the more than 4,500 administrators, staff members, principals, assistant principals, and teachers who participated in interviews and surveys and shared their valuable time and insights with us.

We acknowledge the important contribution of our reviewers. We thank Jim Spillane of Northwestern University and Mark Berends of Vanderbilt University for their thoughtful reviews and comments. We also appreciate the assistance given by Pearson NCS with survey development, administration, and processing. The project could not have been completed without significant support from our RAND colleagues, including Sheila Kirby, Sue Bodilly, Janet Hansen, and Laura Hamilton, who offered valuable input at various stages of the study. We also thank Nancy Rizor for her valued assistance on this report and throughout the project.

Finally, we thank Mike Smith and The William and Flora Hewlett Foundation for their generous support of this research.

Abbreviations

AYP	adequate yearly progress
CFC	Content-Focused Coaching^{SM}
CGCS	Council of the Great City Schools
DL	Disciplinary Literacy
ELA	English language arts
ELL	English language learner
IFL	Institute for Learning
LEP	limited English proficient
LRDC	Learning Research and Development Center
NAEP	National Assessment of Educational Progress
NCLB	No Child Left Behind Act
PD	professional development
POLs	Principles of Learning
SIP	School Improvement Plan/Planning

CHAPTER ONE

Introduction

In the past decade, the responsibilities facing school district central offices have greatly increased. They now include not only management and personnel duties, but also oversight of school improvement, facilitation of community engagement, and provision of professional development. The current high-stakes accountability environment brought on by the federal No Child Left Behind Act (NCLB) adds enormous pressure on districts to perform these roles well and to demonstrate success. The threat of sanctions for districts and schools failing to demonstrate improved student achievement places even greater demands on central office administrators to provide teachers and administrators with the skills, knowledge, and resources needed to help all students meet high academic standards. These pressures are escalating rapidly as states ratchet up their progress targets to meet the federal goal of academic proficiency for all students by 2014. Unless the federal government or states alter NCLB rules or targets—and many have this past year—it will become even more difficult for districts and their schools to meet these accountability expectations over time.

In the national drive to raise student achievement, urban school districts face major challenges:

- Despite some improvement in recent years, achievement levels remain relatively low in urban districts, even when controlling for their level of poverty.[1]
- Most urban districts struggle to attract and retain a well-qualified teaching force. For example, research shows that high-poverty public schools have a significantly higher teacher turn-over rate (20 percent) than more-affluent public schools (12 percent) (Ingersoll, 2001, 2003).
- There is rapid leadership turnover in these settings. For example, in 2003, the average tenure of superintendents in urban districts belonging to the Council of the Great City Schools (CGCS) was 2.75 years (CGCS, 2003).
- Large urban districts enroll the majority of poor, minority, and immigrant children in the country.[2]
- Despite serving a more disadvantaged population, urban schools spend close to the national average per pupil, and their expenditures have been increasing less rapidly than average expenditures nationally (CGCS, 2000, 2004; Quality Counts, 1998).
- Many central offices lack the personnel and staff expertise and skills needed to bring about systemwide improvement.

Given their limited capacity, many districts look to outside organizations for assistance. In recent years, an increasing number of organizations have emerged to address this need, ranging from orga-

---

[1] For example, on the 1994 National Assessment of Educational Progress (NAEP) reading test, only 23 percent of fourth graders in high-poverty urban schools achieved at the basic level or above. This statistic compares with 46 percent of students in high-poverty schools in nonurban areas; in nonpoverty schools, 69 percent of fourth graders were ranked at the basic level and above (Quality Counts, 1998). Similarly, although a more recent analysis of state assessment results in 61 city school systems found gains in math and reading performance and some signs of reduction in racially identifiable achievement gaps, urban schools as a group still scored below state and national averages (CGCS, 2004).

[2] The 100 largest urban districts, representing less than 1 percent of all districts in the country, educate 23 percent of all public school children, approximately 40 percent of all non-white students, and 30 percent of students receiving free and reduced-price lunches (MDRC, 2003). In these 100 districts, 69 percent of students were nonwhite, compared to 41 percent in all school districts; 54 percent were eligible for free and reduced-price lunches, compared to 40 percent of students in all districts (National Center for Education Statistics, 2003).

nizations working with districts nationally to those working on a local level. Many of these organizations have gained prominence and support from private foundations; most notably, the Annenberg Challenge grant was a catalyst for many (Kronley and Handley, 2003). These external organizations—sometimes called "nonsystem actors" (Cohen, 1995), intermediaries (Bodilly, 2001; Honig, 2004), or reform support organizations (Kronley and Handley, 2003)—generally seek to support "system reform." As opposed to technical assistance or professional development providers supporting one facet of an organization, these intermediaries envision a more comprehensive transformation of the organization and seek to build the capacity of school and central office staff to support improvements in teaching and learning.

Study Purpose

In fall 2002, RAND initiated a formative assessment of three urban districts' efforts to improve the instructional quality and performance of their schools. The study also sought to assess the contribution to these efforts made by one intermediary organization, the Institute for Learning (IFL). The IFL seeks to support district instructional improvement through the provision of technical assistance, networking opportunities, knowledge and research, materials and tools, and advice for district leaders. As we discuss in the next two chapters, the IFL is not an intervention or model that districts implemented. Rather, it is a reform partner that coaches and assists districts with various aspects of instructional reform and tailors its work to each local context. Therefore, we did not seek to evaluate the IFL in a traditional sense—as one might do in a study of a particular school reform model (e.g., Success for All). Instead, we started from the perspective of the districts and their reform efforts and sought to understand the role of the IFL in supporting district reform.

The immediate purpose of this research was to provide feedback to the three districts and the IFL to improve their reform efforts. While a sample of three districts limits the generalizability of our findings, the study nonetheless offers other policymakers, funders, and administrators important insights about how to improve teaching and learning in urban districts. Such improvement is critical to any attempt to erase the achievement gap between students of different racial and socioeconomic backgrounds and to achieving the goals of NCLB. As such, the efforts of these three urban districts, as well as the IFL's conception of a strategy for improving schools in urban districts, shed light on strategies for improvement, outcomes associated with implementation, and challenges urban districts and intermediaries face in attempting to bring about systemwide change.

Overall, the study addressed the following questions:

1. What strategies did districts employ to promote instructional improvement? How did these strategies work?
2. What were the constraints and enablers of district instructional improvement efforts?
3. What was the impact of the IFL? What were the constraints and enablers of the district-IFL partnerships?
4. What are the implications for district instructional improvement and district-intermediary partnerships?

Methodology

As described in more detail in the next chapter, we used a comparative case study design and mixed methods to answer these questions. We collected and analyzed data from extensive field interviews and focus groups conducted over a two-year period; from surveys of elementary, middle, and high school principals and teachers; from district and IFL documents; and from demographic and student achievement databases.

Organization of the Report

In Chapter Two, we present a brief review of the literature on school district reform and intermediary organizations, along with the conceptual framework and methodology of the study. Chapter Three provides an overview and background on the three study districts and the Institute for Learning. Chapter Four analyzes and describes the design, implementation, and selected intermediate outcomes of key instructional improvement strategies pursued in the three districts—laying the groundwork for a broader analysis of cross-case and cross-reform-strategy findings presented in the subsequent chapter. Chapter Five identifies cross-cutting themes and key factors that constrained and enabled district reform, and Chapter Six provides evidence on the impact of the IFL on district instructional reform efforts and the factors influencing the effectiveness of the partnerships. The final chapter summarizes the overarching findings of the study and provides tentative lessons for policy and practice.

CHAPTER TWO

Research Background, Framework, and Methods

In this chapter, we review the literature in which we grounded the study and its conceptual framework. We then describe in detail our framework and methodology for collecting and analyzing data on district reform and partnership efforts.

What We Know from Prior Research

The framework for this study is grounded in the research on school district instructional change and on intermediary organizations. We reviewed these two literature bases with two specific goals in mind: to situate the particular organizations we studied in a broader context and to help develop a framework to guide our data collection and analysis.

School Districts and Instructional Improvement
A growing body of research has documented the key roles that districts play in supporting improvements in teaching and learning—building a strong case that school district central offices could and should be instruments for significant reform on a wide scale (David, 1990; Massell and Goertz, 1999; Rosenholtz, 1989; Spillane, 1996, 1997). The work of New York City's Community District 2 is often cited as proof that districts have the capacity to be agents of instructional improvement (Elmore and Burney, 1999). This research has also identified preconditions and strategies associ-

ated with "success" (Elmore and Burney, 1999; Fullan, 2000; High-tower et al., 2002; Massell, 2000; Massell and Goertz, 1999; McLaughlin and Talbert, 2002; Rosenholtz, 1989; Snipes et al., 2002; Togneri and Anderson, 2003; for a review of research, see Marsh, 2002).[1] Collectively, this literature suggests the following attributes of reforming districts:

- A strong focus on teaching, learning, and instructional improvement, which is supported by clear expectations and sustained over time
- A systemwide approach to reform: conceptualizing strategies with all aspects of the system in mind and with an understanding that individuals at all levels are responsible for change
- Alignment and coherence of policies (e.g., alignment of curriculum with standards and instruction)
- Strong support for teacher learning and professional development, including the pursuit of cutting-edge or new approaches to professional development
- The use of data to drive decisions and instruction and to hold schools accountable
- Support for developing the instructional leadership of principals and others.

Several other studies find that reforming districts offer targeted support for low-performing schools (Massell, 2000; Massell and Goertz,

---

[1] The authors cited herein vary in their definitions of success. Some base success on student outcomes, such as Snipes et al. (2002), who examined districts demonstrating trends of improved student achievement and improvement that outpaced statewide gains, and Togneri and Anderson (2003), who analyzed districts that exhibited at least three years of improved student achievement across grades, subjects, and racial/ethnic groups. Others focused on districts that were reform-oriented—for example, Rosenholtz (1989), who compared "moving" districts (those that provided a clear focus on instruction and encouraged educators to take risks) with "stuck" districts (those with fragmented instructional goals and policies); and Massell (2000), who examined the capacity-building activities of 22 districts and focused on districts that "embraced these activities in a more comprehensive way and use them as major mechanisms for enacting improvement" (p. 1). The studies cited also vary in their methods and rigor. Thus, there is no solid evidence base proving that a certain set of district-level factors leads to improved student outcomes.

1999; Snipes et al., 2002) and gradually phase in instructional reform efforts (Elmore and Burney, 1999; Snipes et al., 2002).

Intermediary Organizations and District Reform

All this research has placed greater attention on systemwide change and the role of school districts. At the same time, researchers, policymakers, and practitioners have also acknowledged the many responsibilities and challenges faced by districts—responsibilities and challenges heightened by new accountability policies. With limited internal capacity and increasing external pressure, many school districts have recognized that they need assistance to bring about meaningful change and have sought external partners—referred to as *intermediaries* in this report—to help them meet these demands and build a coherent instructional focus across their system of schools.[2]

The literature on intermediaries, albeit "thin," generally conceives of these organizations as mediating, building capacity, and bridging gaps. According to one researcher,

> Intermediaries are organizations that occupy the space *in between* at least two other parties. Intermediary organizations' primary function is *to mediate* or to manage change for both those parties. Intermediary organizations operate independently of these two parties and provide distinct value for those parties beyond what the parties alone would be able to develop or to amass by themselves. At the same time, intermediaries depend on those parties to perform their essential functions. (Honig, 2004, p. 67)

Kronley and Handley (2003, p. 4) defined these groups as "outside organizations—public, quasi-public, private for-profit, and private nonprofit—that seek to engage or are engaged by school districts and

---

[2] A recent report by the National Clearinghouse for Comprehensive School Reform and the Annenberg Institute for School Reform, the Consortium for Policy Research in Education, and New American Schools recommends that districts "invest in outside expertise . . . to obtain technical help for supporting district staff during the reform process" (p. 18) and "develop partnerships with reform support organizations to redesign the district leadership structure and make it more efficient and beneficial to schools and employees" (Martinez and Harvey, 2004; p. 20).

efforts at systemic reform." According to these authors, such organizations support a process of transformation that seeks to bring about better outcomes for students. Other authors emphasize the variety of roles that intermediary organizations play: advocacy (e.g., prodding systems to improve, building public support for change), technical assistance (e.g., providing training), and gap-fillers (e.g., augmenting insufficient financial, human, or intellectual resources) (Corcoran and Lawrence, 2003; Rothman, 2003).

Some researchers have argued that intermediaries are advantageous reform partners because of their ability to complement district limitations. For example, unlike districts, intermediaries are often less constrained by political pressures and bureaucratic structures, which are seen as slowing response time, stymieing innovation, and leading to inertia in typical districts. Intermediaries also have a more concentrated focus, so they can focus solely on instruction—unlike districts, which must focus on a broad array of areas that include transportation and personnel. Finally, intermediaries can serve as a source of stability and institutional memory in districts where leadership turnover is frequent (Corcoran, 2003; Rothman, 2003; Vargo, 2004; Vargo and Toussaint, 2002).

In recent years, researchers have identified dimensions along which various types of intermediary organizations vary, including location relative to the district (i.e., local versus imported), the extent to which the intermediary is tied to a specific theory or approach, funding sources, types of organizations between which intermediaries mediate, membership or position of intermediary staff, and scope of work (Honig, 2004; Kronley and Handley, 2003). One of the few national, cross-case studies of intermediary organizations and their work with districts found significant differences among the intermediaries studied not only along these dimensions, but also regarding the origin, purpose, modes of operation, budgets, beliefs, expectations, methods of assessment, and duration of work (Kronley and Handley, 2003).

A handful of studies have documented the impacts of intermediary organizations on district reform. One study of local intermediaries in a California school district found that such organizations filled district resource gaps in three key areas: disseminating and building knowledge, forging social and political ties, and building infrastructure (Honig, 2004). Similarly, a study of a business-sponsored, imported intermediary working in four school districts for more than ten years found that the intermediary enhanced district capacity to support improvements in instruction. In particular, researchers found altered leadership (new norms, learning communities), greater coherence in policies, increased access to materials and tools, changes in the scope and nature of professional development, changes in professional culture, and greater attention to data for decisionmaking (Corcoran and Lawrence, 2003). The national, cross-case study cited above also provided some anecdotal evidence on several "measures of interim success" in the districts examined, including the development of a shared language, the emergence of new or altered roles for individuals at various levels, and a recognition that "what began as an innovation has become a habit of being" (Kronley and Handley, 2003, p. 55).

Conceptual Framework

Our study is guided by a conceptual framework that describes the instructional improvement efforts of districts engaged in partnership with an intermediary organization. We developed this framework in two parts. First, we drew on existing literature to develop a general notion or theory of action for district reform and the contextual factors that might influence these efforts. Second, our first year of exploratory data collection allowed us to specify this generic theory of action to reflect the specific actions taken and outcomes expected in the three study districts. As a result, our conceptual framework is a hybrid model, which we derived in part from the literature and then refined as we began to collect and analyze data.

As Figure 2.1 illustrates, the framework begins by describing the districts' theory of change for promoting instructional improvement. Although district work includes areas other than instructional improvement, this study focuses on district efforts to promote improvements in teaching and learning.

Figure 2.1
Conceptual Framework

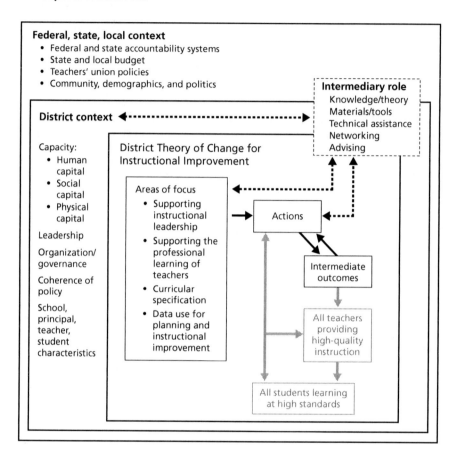

The district's theory of change for instructional improvement starts from district decisions to focus time, energy, and other resources within certain *key areas*. The decision to focus on these areas may be in response to state or federal legislation, or based on a particular deficiency district leaders identified as needing attention, or chosen as a result of the district's relationship with an outside partner such as the IFL. Similar to the findings identified in recent research on reforming districts, each of the districts in this study invested in four key areas:[3]

- *Supporting instructional leadership.* Instructional leaders are knowledgeable about instruction and therefore able to lead, support, and hold teachers accountable for implementation of standards, curriculum reforms, and other instructional improvement initiatives.
- *Supporting the professional learning of teachers, with a particular focus on school-based coaching in two districts.* On-site instructional experts in schools provide teachers with training and other assistance in improving instructional practice and implementing school- and/or district-based initiatives.
- *Specifying and providing greater guidance on standards-based curricula.* Guidance includes standards-aligned documents that specify timelines and sequencing for covering content throughout the school year, as well as supporting materials such as assessments and sample lesson plans.
- *Using data for planning and instructional improvement.* Administrators and teachers are encouraged to inform instructional decisions by means of data or evidence that is systematically collected to measure the quantity and quality of education practice and outcomes and factors affecting them. These data may include test results; information on student graduation, attendance, and discipline; survey results; systematic reviews of student work; and observational information on classroom practice.

The study analyzed specific reform efforts within each of these four focal areas (see Table 2.1 on page 16 for specific actions taken).

The district theory of change posits that the decision to focus efforts within one or more key areas led each district to take various *actions* or *strategies*, such as establishing a policy or program, as a

---

[3] All three districts also targeted support to low-performing schools. Given that many of these strategies fell into the other four categories (e.g., extra support for data use in low-performing schools), we have chosen not to discuss this as a separate area of focus.

means for effecting change within each priority area. District leaders expected these actions to lead to a set of *intermediate outcomes* that were then expected to affect the quality of instruction throughout the district and ultimately lead to improved student learning. For example, in the area of supporting effective instructional leadership, districts may have taken actions such as redefining principal responsibilities, providing additional training, or instituting a new evaluation tool that focused on instructional leadership. As a result of actions such as these, districts expected certain intermediate outcomes to occur, for example, greater knowledge about high-quality instruction on the part of principals or the establishment of a common language around instruction throughout the district. District leaders viewed these intermediate outcomes as the means through which improvements in teaching and learning would eventually occur. The feedback arrows in the diagram's inner box indicate that these pathways were often bidirectional, showing that certain outcomes often led district leaders to revise initial actions or strategies.

The conceptual framework also recognizes that instructional improvement efforts existed within a broader *district context*, which in turn resided within a larger *federal, state, and local context*—all of which potentially influenced the design, implementation, and impact of district instructional improvement efforts. For example, past studies have shown that various dimensions of district capacity—human capital (e.g., level of staffing, the knowledge, skills, and will of staff), physical capital (e.g., time, materials), and social capital (e.g., trust, normative culture)—can greatly affect district reform efforts (Burch and Spillane, 2004; Bryk and Schneider, 2002; Elmore and Burney, 1999; Firestone, 1989; McLaughlin, 1992; Spillane and Thompson, 1997; Togneri and Anderson, 2003; see Marsh 2002 for detailed review). Similarly, the nature and stability of district leadership and organization (Berends, Bodilly, and Kirby, 2002; Bodilly, 1998; Corcoran, Fuhrman, and Belcher, 2001; McLaughlin, 1992; Snipes et al., 2002; Spillane, 1998; Togneri and Anderson, 2003), as well as state and federal policies, may have also affected the direction of work in districts.

Finally, the framework highlights the role of intermediary organizations, such as the IFL, in attempting to support districts by providing *knowledge, materials, technical assistance, networking opportunities*, and high-level *advice* to district leaders.[4] Building on existing literature, we hypothesize that these resources could affect various aspects of this model, including the district's overall capacity to lead reform or the design and implementation of specific actions. As such, the IFL may have influenced districts' decisions on where to focus their efforts and how to conceptualize the set of strategies, as well as the enactment of those strategies. The bidirectional nature of the arrows also implies that the IFL potentially learned from its work with districts and altered its own practices or theories based on these experiences.

Table 2.1 specifies the specific instructional improvement actions and intermediate outcomes examined in this study. Although this table provides a comprehensive list of the actions and outcomes district leaders associated with implementing reform strategies within each key area of reform, we focus on the most salient actions and outcomes, as well as those we were best able to measure (discussed further in Chapter Four). Our study design did not allow us to link these reforms to the final outcomes of improved teaching and learning. Thus, in the context of this study, we define *progress* as meeting the intermediate goals outlined in Table 2.1.

---

[4] We chose not to frame the larger conceptual framework from the perspective of the IFL for several reasons. Although the IFL has developed a theory of action for its work, that theory did not exist at the outset of IFL's partnerships with the three study districts. Further, the IFL's theory of action has changed from year to year since its development and would have been difficult to use as a conceptual guide. Finally, as noted earlier, given that the IFL operates more as a coach than as a standardized model that districts implement, we chose to frame the study from the perspective of the districts, with the intent of understanding the contribution of the IFL to districts' reform plans and actions.

Table 2.1
Mapping of Actions and Intermediate Outcomes

Actions	Intermediate Outcomes
Supporting Instructional Leadership	
Professional development (PD) seminars	Principals:
Instructionally focused principal meetings	• are knowledgeable about instruction
Instructionally focused supervision of principals	• provide support for teachers (e.g., consultants, coaching)
Revision of hiring criteria for principals	• provide feedback to teachers
New or revised evaluation processes for principals	• conduct classroom observations
District-based preparation programs for principals	• emphasize instruction (e.g., in faculty meetings, evaluations)
Support for principals to attend IFL meetings in Pittsburgh	• design or deliver PD
	• review student work and student data to make decisions about how to improve instruction
	• hold teachers accountable for making improvements in instruction
School-Based Coaching	
Newly created position and defined role	Coaches:
Recruitment and hiring	• act as instructional leaders at the school level
Communication of purpose	Teachers:
PD for coaches	• are knowledgeable about instruction
Encouragement or mandated revision of school schedules	• are trained to implement specific district initiatives
Redefined teacher PD in relation to coach's role	• value interactions with coaches
	• value PD
	• value collaboration
	• collaborate frequently
	Common language in use around larger instructional initiatives
	Consistent messages received about instructional priorities, strategies, practices

Table 2.1—continued

Actions	Intermediate Outcomes
Curriculum Specification	
Curriculum guides aligned with state standards and assessments	Teachers: • value guides for curriculum planning
PD on curriculum guides	• feel prepared to use guides
Staff tasked to support use (e.g., coaches, specialists)	• regularly use guides to plan instruction • feel better able to prepare students for state assessments
Supporting materials for guides • assessments aligned with the guides	Principals: • value guides for monitoring instruction
Adoption of curriculum packages and materials	• regularly use them to monitor instruction
	Common language in use around larger instructional initiatives
	Consistent messages received about instructional priorities, strategies, practices
Data Use for Instructional Improvement	
School improvement planning	Data are accessible to administration and teachers
District assessments	
Data systems	Data are perceived to be useful for instructional decisions
Technical assistance to schools on data use	Data are used for instructional decisions
PD on data use	Individuals at all levels are familiar with and better able to identify areas of need
Learning Walks	
Encouragement of review of student work	

Methods

The study employed a comparative case study design to examine the ways in which instructional improvement efforts and district-intermediary partnerships played out in multiple district settings. We drew on a mix of qualitative and quantitative data in three study districts. The following section provides further details on the district sample and data sources.

Sample

We conducted the study in a purposive sample of three school districts—Monroe, Roosevelt, and Jefferson.[5] From the limited number of IFL partner districts, we chose these three based on several factors: district-IFL partnerships that were more established (i.e., the IFL had been working with these districts for at least three years); prioritization of districtwide instructional improvement by district leaders; district size, union environment, and state context to allow for relevant comparisons; and willingness to participate (all three welcomed the feedback we provided through annual briefings).

Data Sources

To analyze the instructional improvement efforts and district-IFL partnerships in these three districts, we collected both qualitative and quantitative data from multiple sources over a two-year period (the 2002–03 and 2003–04 school years). The following section describes each data source.

District Site Visits with Fieldwork. Researchers visited each district twice during the 2002–03 school year and three to four times during the 2003–04 school year, with each visit lasting approximately one week. During the first visit, we sampled a similar set of individuals to interview in each district based on a generic set of job descriptions for individuals likely to be responsible for or able to influence district instructional policies and programs. In subsequent visits, researchers often employed snowballing techniques in which interviewees nominated other individuals for interviews. During both years, we interviewed central office leaders and staff—including the superintendent, associate superintendents, and administrators in the areas of curriculum, instruction, and professional development—to understand reform priorities and the nature of policies, programs, and work with the IFL. Interviews with community leaders, such as school board members and union officials, also provided critical contextual

---

[5] To ensure anonymity, we used pseudonyms for the names of the districts. In addition, statistics cited about the districts and communities are approximations, not exact figures.

information. As Table 2.2 illustrates, we conducted a total of 85 interviews with district and community leaders.

In spring 2003 and winter-spring 2004, we visited a sample of schools in each district, representing a range of grade levels, demographic characteristics, and student performance levels (see Appendix A for further description). During the 2003 school visits, we interviewed principals in all three districts and, in Roosevelt and Jefferson, conducted focus group discussions with teachers to understand how district and IFL actions played out at the school and classroom levels.[6] During school visits in the second year of data collection, researchers interviewed the principal, and where relevant, assistant principal(s) and coach(es), and conducted one to three focus group discussions with teachers. During both years, we worked with school leaders to select teachers representing a range of grade levels and years of experience. Finally, in each district we observed several district-

Table 2.2
District Site Visit Interviews and Focus Groups (2003 and 2004)

	Central Office and Community	Schools				
	No. of Interviews	No. of School Visits	No. of Principal Interviews	No. of Assistant Principal Interviews	No. of Coach Interviews	No. of Teacher Focus Groups
Monroe	36	33	33	18	10	43
Jefferson	28	19	18	7	16	39
Roosevelt	21	20	21	5	24	36
Total	85	72	73	30	50	118

NOTES: Monroe school visits in 2003 involved principal interviews only. Counts for Monroe school interviews and focus groups with other school staff pertain to 2004 only.

---

[6] Because of the large number of schools in Monroe, researchers elected to visit twice as many schools in 2003 in an effort to speak to principals from a wider range of schools across the district. Our limited study resources, however, precluded us from conducting teacher focus groups in the schools visited in 2003.

sponsored meetings and professional development sessions, as well as IFL activities conducted in the districts.

IFL Site Visits with Fieldwork. To better understand the work of the IFL, the research team conducted interviews and focus groups with Institute leaders and staff during both years—including the director, the executive director, and the IFL resident fellow(s) assigned to each of the study districts and to other districts. In total, we spoke to 18 individuals, often several times over the course of the study. We also observed IFL meetings in Pittsburgh and Chicago.

Document Review. Throughout the course of the study, researchers collected documents pertaining to district instructional reform efforts, such as district improvement plans, curriculum guides, professional development schedules, job descriptions, evaluation tools, and school board meeting minutes. To understand IFL arrangements and work with districts, we collected the IFL's written plans, meeting agendas, trademarked materials (e.g., CDs, manuals), letters, and other documents pertaining to IFL activities.

Principal and Teacher Surveys. In spring 2004, we surveyed all principals in the three districts, all teachers in Jefferson and Roosevelt, and a sample of teachers in Monroe to further assess the implementation of policies and programs within the four areas, the expected intermediate outcomes, and exposure to IFL ideas and practices.[7] Appendix A presents generic copies of the principal and teacher survey instruments (i.e., stripped of identifying district information and terminology). Appendix B provides additional details about survey sampling and methods. As Table 2.3 illustrates, the majority of principals responded to the survey, whereas a much smaller proportion of teachers responded. Although our analysis indicates that both principal and teacher respondents were reasonably

---

[7] Monroe administrators requested that we not survey all teachers. As a compromise, we selected a purposive sample of 72 of Monroe's schools (approximately 70 percent of all schools) that included all the middle and high schools and a sample of 44 elementary schools stratified by student performance as measured by state test results. Surveys were sent to up to 43 randomly selected classroom teachers in each school sampled. If a school had fewer than 43 teachers, all teachers were surveyed. See Appendix B for a more detailed description of the sampling framework.

Table 2.3
Survey Response Rates, Spring 2004 (%)

	Principals	Teachers
Monroe	78	48
Jefferson	72	46
Roosevelt	68	31

NOTE: In Monroe, surveys were administered to teachers in a stratified sample of 72 schools (see Appendix B for sampling details).

representative of the larger population, systematic differences could exist between responders and nonresponders. To adjust for potential differences due to nonresponse, we calculated nonresponse weights from a logistic regression, where response status was the dependent variable and independent variables included school level, teacher certification status, number of years of teaching experience, percentage of students who were from low-income families and percentage of students who were nonwhite, and district-specific ratings for school performance status. While these weights may have reduced some of the potential bias, there may be other factors affecting nonresponse for which we were unable to account. As such, survey results reported herein should be interpreted as the relative response of those who responded to the survey and not necessarily representative of all teachers and principals in the study districts. For our analysis, we also weighted the teacher survey data in Monroe to adjust for differences resulting from differential sampling. (See Appendix B for additional details on survey data weights.)

Demographic and Student Achievement Data. For each district, we gathered data on student and teacher characteristics and student performance from the year prior to IFL entry (1997–98) to the final study year (2003–04). We obtained student achievement data from state departments of education, demographic data from the National Center for Education Statistics (Common Core of Data), and teacher data from each study district.

Data Analysis

Site lead researchers for each district analyzed all documents and interview and focus group notes and transcripts along the dimensions outlined in the conceptual framework. They developed analytic memoranda for each school visited and for each district as a whole—memoranda that included extensive excerpts from the more than 350 interviews and focus groups conducted during the study. Team members also analyzed survey data—once again, framed around the elements of the conceptual framework—within and across districts, comparing responses of individuals at different organizational levels where appropriate (e.g., central office versus school; primary versus secondary schools). From these qualitative and quantitative memos and subsequent meetings, the research team integrated findings from the different sources of data to identify cross-district findings and themes regarding the nature, quality, perceived impact, and potential barriers and enablers of district instructional improvement efforts and district-IFL partnerships.

This report summarizes those overarching findings and presents selected survey data and interview excerpts as supporting evidence. Quotes cited herein generally represent typical responses heard in multiple settings or, in some cases, instances in which an individual eloquently articulated a theme that emerged from our analysis.

Finally, it is worth noting that, although we employed a two-year longitudinal design and collected some retrospective data to provide historical context, our analysis does not focus on changes over time. We believed that we did not have sufficient data (e.g., one year of survey data) and that not enough time had elapsed during the study to substantiate major claims about shifts in practice or outcomes.

Study Limitations

The major limitations of our study stem from the limited sample size and data constraints. First, like any study with a sample size of three, the findings presented in this report cannot be generalized to all districts or to all IFL district partnerships. The findings, however, can contribute to the policy conversation on district reform and intermediary organizations. As past research has shown, many districts are attempting reforms in the same four areas emphasized by the three study districts. Thus, findings on what constrained and enabled efforts in these three districts may offer lessons to organizations and policymakers with similar goals and contexts. The study also identifies important issues that future research can pursue in a wider array of settings.

Second, the decision to focus on districts with well-established partnerships with the IFL may have limited the validity of some data. Our information about staff intentions, actions, and outcomes in the beginning years of the IFL-district partnership was less precise because of our reliance on retrospective data. Although we attempted to address the potential limitations of retrospective data by capturing multiple interview accounts of the same events and using documents to confirm and disconfirm interview accounts, we nonetheless were unable to obtain information as valid as it would have been had we been able to conduct interviews at the start of the partnerships.

Third, teacher survey response rates were low, and although we applied weights to minimize the impact of nonresponse, some of the teacher results may not be representative of the entire population. Further limitations of this study stem from the lack of teaching and learning outcome measures, as well as from our inability to establish causal inferences from the data collected. Finally, because of budgetary constraints, we were able to administer surveys only during the final study year. Longitudinal data over a period of years would have enhanced our analysis of intermediate outcomes and provided more precise measures of change over time.

Formative Feedback

At the end of both years of data collection, we gave briefings to each of the three districts and the Institute for Learning. These briefings provided leaders and staff with feedback on the implementation and perceived impact of district and IFL reform efforts at the district and school levels—with specific attention to the design, enactment, and outcomes of instructional improvement efforts in the four common areas, and to the perceived role of the IFL in those efforts. During the second and final briefing, we gave districts descriptive results from the teacher and principal surveys. Our intent was to assist districts and the IFL in the planning and improvement of future reform activities.

CHAPTER THREE

Setting the Stage: Overview of Study Districts and the IFL

Each of the three urban school districts examined in this study—Monroe, Roosevelt, and Jefferson—forged an early partnership with the IFL in the late 1990s or early 2000. This chapter provides an overview and background of the three districts as well as a description of the IFL and its partnership with each district.

The Three Study Districts: Characteristics and Context

As illustrated in Table 3.1, all three study districts were located in urban settings. They all served diverse student populations, the majority of which were low-income and minority.[1] Similarly, all three districts faced significant budget shortfalls in recent years, requiring layoffs and reductions in services. Yet the districts also varied along several key dimensions: size, proportion of at-risk students, union environment, and stability of top leadership. Monroe (located in a southern state) was a larger district, operating in a weak union environment with relatively fewer at-risk students and one superintendent at its helm throughout the duration of the IFL partnership. In contrast, Jefferson and Roosevelt (both located in eastern states) were smaller districts, with stronger union environments and more-frequent lead-

---

[1] Statistics cited in this table and throughout the text have been slightly altered to maintain district anonymity, but basic proportions and scale remain true. Also, to mask the identity of district leaders, we use the masculine pronoun throughout the report.

Table 3.1
Characteristics of Study Districts, 2003–04

Characteristic	Monroe	Roosevelt	Jefferson
Number of students	80,000	30,000	30,000
Number of teachers	5,000	2,000	2,000
Number of schools	100	50	50
Percentage of low-income students[a]	55	80	75
Percentage of minority students	70	85	80
Percentage of Limited English Proficient (LEP) students	20	15	10
Percentage of special education students	10	20	20
Strength of teachers' union	Right-to-work state, weak	Collective bargaining state, strong	Collective bargaining state, strong
School year district-IFL partnership started	1999–2000	1999–2000	1998–99
Number of superintendents since inception of IFL partnership	1	2	3
Percentage of schools identified for improvement or beyond) under NCLB[b]	0	40	40
Percentage of schools at risk of being identified for improvement[b,c]	15	50	20

[a]The definition of low-income varied among the available data in each state. In Monroe, it was defined as the students eligible for free- or reduced-price lunches or other public assistance; in Roosevelt it was defined as students eligible for free- or reduced-price meals, and in Jefferson it was defined as students eligible for free- or reduced-price meals or whose families receive transitional aid to families benefits or are eligible for food stamps.
[b]Based on spring 2003 assessment results and state-defined proficiency targets.
[c]Defined as schools that failed to make adequate yearly progress (AYP) based on spring 2003 assessments but have not failed AYP for two consecutive years.

ership turnover. These two districts also enrolled larger proportions of at-risk students and had higher numbers of schools labeled "low-performing" on state measures.

The districts also varied in the performance of students over time. Both Monroe and Jefferson made substantial progress in increasing the percentage of proficient students from 1997–98 through 2003–04; Roosevelt had more limited success.[2] In addition, while each district performed worse relative to its state average on measures of both percentage of proficient and percentage of low-performing students, the districts had some success in improving the performance of their students over the time period in which they partnered with the IFL. Monroe showed the greatest success. Jefferson and Roosevelt both struggled to reduce the gap between percentage of students proficient in the district and state averages, but both districts achieved some success in reducing the gap between state and district averages in percentage of low-performing students. Appendix B presents a detailed description of this achievement trend analysis. We remind the reader that it is not meant to be a causal analysis relating student achievement to particular district reform efforts or to district partnerships with the IFL. Rather, it provides an overview of performance patterns over the course of time when districts were engaged in IFL partnerships up to the end of this study.

Institute for Learning: Background and History

The three study districts forged partnerships with the Institute for Learning in either the 1998–99 or 1999–2000 school year. The following subsections briefly describe the history and evolution of the IFL as an organization and as a partner in the three districts.

Stage One: Early History and Evolution

In 1996, Dr. Lauren Resnick helped found the Institute for Learning in response to requests from a group of urban school district superintendents for assistance with implementing standards-based teaching. As members of the New Standards movement, these districts were proponents of standards-based teaching and had an established relationship with the IFL's parent organization—the Learning Research

---

[2] The 1997–98 school year was chosen as a starting point because it precedes the point at which each district entered into a partnership with the IFL.

and Development Center (LRDC) at the University of Pittsburgh. LRDC conceived of the IFL as a "think tank" or "iterative research and development process" where research would be translated into usable knowledge for practitioners and where, in turn, practitioners would share lessons learned during implementation to further refine theory. The IFL's goal in engaging in this process was to buck the trend of supporting school-by-school reform and instead to scale up standards-based instruction within urban school districts.

LRDC researchers and IFL developers worked to articulate theories and craft tools, such as a theory of standards-based teaching embodied in a set of Principles of Learning (POLs)[3] generated from research in cognitive psychology (Resnick and Hall, 1998), as well as research conducted in Community District 2 in New York City (Elmore and Burney, 1999). Table 3.2 describes three commonly cited POLs.

Table 3.2
Examples of Principles of Learning

Principle	Description
Clear Expectations	Clear standards of achievement and measures of students' progress toward those standards offer real incentives for students to work hard and succeed. Descriptive criteria and models that meet the standards are displayed in the schools, and the students refer to these displays to help them analyze and discuss their work.
Academic Rigor in a Thinking Curriculum	In every subject, at every grade level, instruction and learning must include commitment to a knowledge core, high thinking demand, and active use of knowledge.
Accountable Talk[SM]	Accountable Talk means using evidence that is appropriate to the discipline and follows established norms of good reasoning. Teachers should create the norms and skills of Accountable Talk in their classrooms.

---

[3] There were originally eight principles: Organizing for Effort, Clear Expectations, Recognition of Accomplishment, Fair and Credible Evaluations, Academic Rigor in a Thinking Curriculum, Accountable Talk, Socializing Intelligence, and Learning as Apprenticeship. The IFL later added a ninth principle, Self-Management of Learning. See Appendix D for detailed descriptions of all POLs.

The IFL also began articulating a theory of instructional leadership that described effective characteristics and behaviors for principals and district leaders, and began developing additional training and tools to support this theory. Most notably, it created protocols and procedures for conducting a *Learning Walk,* which the IFL defines as "an organized walk through a school's halls and classrooms using the POLs to focus on the instructional core" (IFL, 2003).[4]

Stage Two: Shift to On-Site Support and Articulated Notions of High-Performing Districts

By March of 1999, the IFL was working with 11 districts, and several other districts were expressing interest in becoming partners. The IFL developed a model for working with districts in which it sent resident fellows to the district to train principals directly and simultaneously develop the capacities of district leaders. Reflecting on its experiences and ideas about what it would take to scale standards-based teaching across a district, the IFL had come to believe that the school district was the appropriate level at which to build a learning organization,[5] At the same time, however, it was concerned that its ideas were not permeating member districts with sufficient depth to enable standards-based teaching in every classroom in the district. This led the Institute to a greater focus on organizational factors to ensure that the right institutional environments for taking reform to scale existed in each district. The result was the IFL's theory of high-performing school districts. Embodied, in part, by its District Design Principles, this theory outlined steps that a district must take to scale standards-based instruction (Resnick and Glennan, 2002). A revised version of the District Design Principles includes the following:

---

[4] Learning Walks typically involve five- to ten-minute visits to a set of classrooms and focus on teaching and learning—often by questioning students and examining their work—as well as how the school is organized to enable student learning. They are not meant to be stand-alone events or high-stakes evaluations of the work of any individual teacher. Rather, a Learning Walk is an ongoing event that informs schools and district staff about current practice and areas that should be targeted in future professional development.

[5] For a description of the IFL's rationale for working with districts, see Resnick and Glennan (2002).

- Commitment to the concept of effort-based intelligence[6]
- Focus on classroom instruction at every level
- Use of coherent standards, curriculum, assessments, and professional development
- Operation through "nested learning communities" emphasizing
  —Two-way accountability in relations between staff
  —The idea that everyone is a learner
- Continuing professional development, based in schools and linked to the instructional program
- Pervasive use of data in making decisions at all levels
- Routine engagement with parents and community.

While the IFL did not explicitly develop corresponding tools and training around the Design Principles until very recently, it articulated a set of strategies intended to help districts operate in ways consistent with these principles (e.g., developing the instructional leadership skills of principals).

Current Status and Scope of IFL Work

At the time of the study, the IFL was working intensively with 13 member districts and one statewide consortium.[7] For a fee, these districts receive a core program consisting of several services. First, member districts receive on-site technical assistance from one or more resident fellows who travel to the district on a regular basis to work directly with district staff members. IFL staff work in many of its dis-

---

[6] In contrast to an assumption that learning is solely a function of inherited aptitude, *effort-based intelligence* posits that "effort actually *creates* ability, that people *become* smart by working hard at the right kinds of learning tasks" (Resnick, 1995, p. 56). Such a belief recognizes that students can reach high standards provided they are willing to work and are enabled to do so through an effort-oriented education system (e.g., one that holds clear expectations for achievement, celebrates success, provides expert instruction).

[7] An additional sixteen affiliate districts receive a less intensive array of services through participation in the IFL's Instructional Leadership Program, a three-year program designed to help smaller districts develop the leadership skills of its employees. In this model, representatives from the districts meet in Pittsburgh and take on the responsibility for bringing IFL ideas back to their districts.

tricts has centered on Leadership Seminars that provide regular opportunities for principals to engage in professional development activities focused on instructional leadership. Depending on the size of the district, the resident fellows may train principals directly or train district leaders who will train principals. The content of the Leadership Seminars is developed collaboratively with district leaders, but focuses on the POLs and ways for principals to support teachers' classroom instruction.

Second, member districts are invited to participate in national seminars for district leaders. In its effort to build the capacity of district administrators, the IFL hosts seminars in Pittsburgh for superintendents, their deputies, and other central office administrators that allow participants to discuss solutions to district problems, with the ultimate goal of creating high-performing learning communities in their districts. Issues for the seminar are selected in consultation with seminar members and range from school-based professional development to parent and community engagement.

Third, members have the opportunity to send a delegation of district and school leaders to the IFL Annual National Retreat of all member districts. They also gain access to the IFL's web-based electronic materials and other tools, research on learning and reform, and IFL leaders for advice on an as-needed basis.

Thus, the core programs represent not a specific model that districts adopt but instead a set of resources that district and IFL staff jointly use and adapt to advance instructional improvement. One IFL resident fellow compared the IFL's work with districts to that of a flamenco guitarist who organically follows the dancer's movements:

> [I]f you're the flamenco guitarist, you follow the flamenco dancer, the dancer does not follow the music. . . . That's what I'm trying to do. I have a body of work, I have a contract with the district that says we will accomplish all of this, but I'm trying to do it in a way that follows [district leader] and follows the teachers and follows [district leaders] . . . instead of having a set way on how we're going to [work]. . . . [I]t isn't a module that's coming off your shelf or out of the file cabinet.

Similarly, district leaders recognize that the IFL is not an organization bringing a reform package to be implemented. Instead, it provides an array of ideas, opportunities, and individuals to assist them with reform. As one district superintendent noted, "It is a complex thing and that's why this is not an intervention. It's kind of a philosophy and a set of tools and procedures, but how you apply it, where you apply it, I see as having like a high inference. . . . [T]here's a lot of flexibility in that."

In addition to the core programs for members and affiliates, the IFL also gives partner districts the option to purchase additional IFL services. One such additional service is Content-Focused Coaching[SM] (CFC), a professional development model in which coaches are trained to work with teachers in schools. The model, grounded in research on teaching and learning (West and Staub, 2003), aims to develop teachers' practice and provide them with the support they need to deliver and reflect on rigorous, standards-based lessons. A second additional service is Disciplinary Literacy (DL), a program that targets secondary teachers and provides skills to discipline-based teachers (English language arts [ELA], history, mathematics, and science) on how to teach the reading, reasoning, investigating, speaking, and writing competencies that students need for gaining complex knowledge in particular academic areas.

IFL-District Partnerships in the Case Study Districts

The three districts examined in this study participated as full members with the Institute for Learning for more than three years each. Even though each district received a similar set of core services, the partnerships evolved in very different ways, depending on the local context and how the individual IFL resident fellows and district leaders decided to focus and shape the IFL work over time. Brief descriptions of each partnership are included below.

Monroe

In January 2000, Monroe's superintendent decided to utilize the IFL to help focus on improving instruction across all schools in the district. The IFL work initially concentrated on large group sessions aimed at central office leaders, staff, and school principals. Jointly led by the IFL lead resident fellow and district administrators, these sessions focused on the theory of effort-based intelligence, building awareness of POLs and other IFL ideas across the district, and utilizing Learning Walks. IFL staff developed professional development modules for district leaders to use in helping principals understand and use IFL ideas and strategies, which principals were then expected to use with their teachers during campus professional development sessions. This "turnkey" approach became the model for spreading the ideas and strategies across the district.

Over the next few years the position of lead resident fellow turned over several times and the focus of IFL work evolved to meet district needs and capitalize on the strengths of fellows. Although POLs and Learning Walks remained central organizing tools, their application changed over the years from a focus on literacy to one on math, and from elementary to secondary instruction. Toward the end of the third year of Monroe's relationship with the IFL, several new districtwide initiatives began to compete with the IFL for time and attention. Indeed, in the following year, many reported waning IFL activities as the new curriculum guides and assessments gained major districtwide focus. In the final study year, the IFL partnership experienced another transition or, as some reported, "a revival," focusing on a district-identified area of need: instruction of English language learners (ELLs). A new resident fellow worked with district leaders to co-develop new systemwide policies for ELLs and provided direct training to a small group of teachers, as well as some principals.

Over the years, the relationship between the IFL and Monroe took many forms. The frequent changes in the lead resident fellow assigned to the district, combined with new district initiatives and needs, shaped and reshaped IFL-district activities each year. In addtion, lessons learned throughout the years produced adjustments to *who* was directly included in IFL activities (e.g., including curriculum staff who had been initially left out) and *how* those activities were conducted (e.g., moving from large-group to small-group training). Even with shifts in IFL activities, there is some evidence to suggest that district personnel worked closely to co-construct the IFL work in Monroe and were taking ownership of the ideas, especially in the later years.

Roosevelt

In 1999, Roosevelt's School Board hired a new superintendent who consulted with the IFL in developing his vision of reform in Roosevelt. He explicitly incorporated IFL theories, ideas, and language into Roosevelt's strategic plan and requested that the IFL send a lead resident fellow to Roosevelt to directly train all principals in the district. In the first year, this lead fellow developed and provided monthly trainings for principals and trained both principals and central office leaders to conduct Learning Walks. In the absence of a director of professional development and curriculum in the district, the lead fellow also performed some of the planning responsibilities of this role and advised top leaders.

Over the next few years, the IFL continued to provide monthly seminars that primarily targeted principals but sometimes included district administrators and assistant principals. In addition, Roosevelt contracted with the IFL to provide its newly hired literacy coaches with training in Content-Focused Coaching^{SM}. The IFL's Disciplinary Literacy work was also being developed and piloted in Roosevelt during the 2000–01 school year. Following a change in superintendents in August 2002 and a reorganization of district leadership, Roosevelt staff began to take on more leadership over several district policies and initiatives—increasingly making decisions without direct IFL influence. In the final study year, the central office administrators began designing and running the principal leadership seminars without IFL support. Roosevelt, however, continued its partnership with the IFL by contracting for CFC and DL training.

Overall, the IFL's partnership with Roosevelt has been relatively comprehensive. The district originally sought the IFL's theories about learning communities, instructional leadership, and Principles of Learning but also heavily invested in all components of the IFL's services as they were made available. In addition, Roosevelt benefited from the stability of having only two lead resident fellows during the first four years of the partnership.

Jefferson

In the 1998–99 school year, Jefferson's superintendent decided to engage in an exploratory process with the IFL, sending district representatives to Institute meetings to investigate whether the district should enter into a more formal partnership with the IFL. During this year, the superintendent implemented some aspects or interpretations of IFL practices—most notably, the Learning Walk—without much support or oversight by the IFL. As a result, the early impressions of the IFL's work by many individuals in the district were not entirely consistent with the Institute's ideas, and many teachers and principals felt rushed into activities they were not adequately prepared for, causing ill feelings about the IFL on the part of many district staff members and union leaders.

At the end of this first year, the superintendent entered into a formal relationship with the IFL. However, the history of the exploratory year led to a rocky start to the relationship—the effects of which are still felt in the district to some degree. Further, with the departure of the superintendent responsible for introducing the IFL into the district and his replacement by a superintendent from outside the district with less prior knowledge of the IFL's ideas, the district's partnership with the IFL stalled and continued to struggle to overcome the inconsistencies and frustrations characteristic of its early years.

Although this early work in the district got off to an inauspicious start, the district maintained a formal relationship with the IFL up to and throughout the course of this study. Over the first four years of the formal partnership, the role of the IFL was primarily that of a professional development provider for school and district leaders, often leading seminar and small study groups and focusing on the

POLs and Learning Walks. In addition, Jefferson piloted the IFL's Disciplinary Literacy program and continued to implement it in a small number of schools.

In the final study year, the IFL's role changed dramatically, moving away from pull-out principal trainings to assistance with the district's efforts to support low-performing schools (e.g., helping to lead guided Learning Walks). The IFL also played a minor role in providing professional development for principals and school-based coaches.

In summary, leadership changes at the district level and confusion about and/or resistance to IFL ideas and practices characterized much of the IFL's relationship with Jefferson. The IFL nonetheless played a consistent role in providing training and support to principals and district administrators. While buy-in to IFL ideas reportedly varied at all levels of the district for the duration of the partnership, district staff appeared to assume greater ownership of IFL ideas in the final study year.

Summary

As described in this chapter, the three study districts have varied in size, student population, union environment, stability of top leadership, and student performance over time. Monroe was a larger district, with relatively smaller proportions of low-income and minority students. The district operates in a weak union context and had one superintendent throughout the duration of the IFL partnership. Compared with the other two districts, Monroe also demonstrated slightly more consistent, positive student achievement gains over time. Jefferson and Roosevelt enroll fewer total students but serve larger proportions of at-risk students and have higher numbers of low-performing schools. These districts also operate in stronger union environments and experience more frequent leadership turnover. Despite these similarities, Jefferson demonstrated more positive student achievement trends than did Roosevelt.

All three districts forged early partnerships with the Institute for Learning, which has evolved significantly as an organization since its inception in 1996. As full members, all three districts received a similar "package" of services, including technical assistance from resident fellows; opportunities to attend meetings; access to research, theory, materials, and tools; and advice from IFL leaders. Nevertheless, the IFL varied greatly in how it initiated partnerships with each district, how it focused its work, the strategies it undertook to support instructional improvement across the three districts, and the intensity of these efforts. With this background in mind, we turn next to an analysis of the instructional reform efforts undertaken in the three study districts.

CHAPTER FOUR

District Strategies to Improve Instruction: Implementation and Outcomes

Our study focused on district instructional improvement efforts in four key areas: promoting the instructional leadership of principals, supporting teacher professional development through the use of school-based coaches, specifying districtwide curricula, and promoting the use of data for instructional decisionmaking. Whereas Table 2.1 provided a comprehensive list of district actions and intermediate outcomes for each key area of district reform, the current chapter describes the most salient district actions within each area, the results of those actions, and the factors that constrained or enabled these efforts. Each section concludes with a brief discussion of the IFL's role in supporting district work within each area. These detailed descriptions lay the groundwork for a broader analysis of cross-district and cross-reform themes and findings presented in Chapters Five and Six.

Although each of the study districts pursued strategies in all four areas of instructional improvement, they tended to focus their efforts on two areas. Interestingly, however, each district chose a unique pair of areas to emphasize. Figure 4.1 describes the relative level of emphasis of each district's actions in the four key areas. First, compared with the investment of resources in the other areas, all three districts placed a moderate amount of emphasis on promoting *instructional leadership*—particularly through professional development and instructionally focused principal supervision. Second, the use of school-based *coaching* was a strong emphasis in two of the districts. Third, while all three districts developed districtwide *curriculum guides*, Monroe and Roosevelt invested significantly more attention

Figure 4.1
Emphasis of District Instructional Improvement Actions

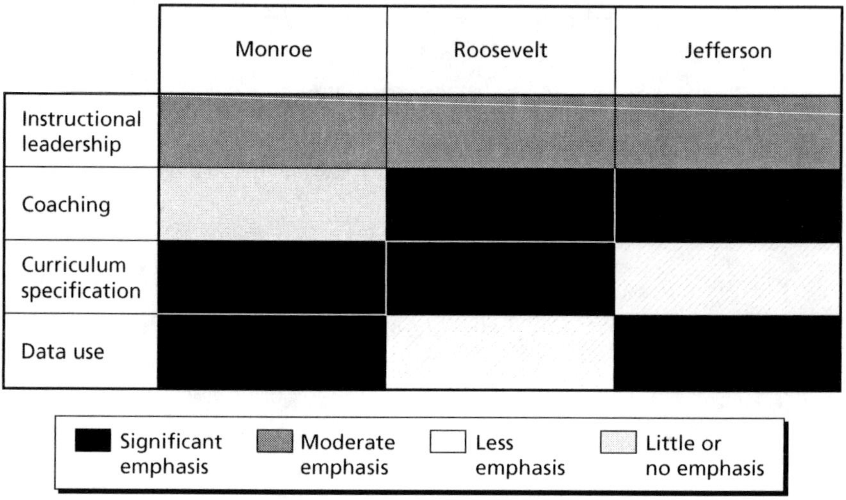

	Monroe	Roosevelt	Jefferson
Instructional leadership	Moderate emphasis	Moderate emphasis	Moderate emphasis
Coaching	Less emphasis	Significant emphasis	Significant emphasis
Curriculum specification	Significant emphasis	Significant emphasis	Little or no emphasis
Data use	Significant emphasis	Less emphasis	Significant emphasis

Legend: ■ Significant emphasis   ▨ Moderate emphasis   ☐ Less emphasis   ☐ Little or no emphasis

and resources in the development, monitoring, and implementation of these guides. Finally, the *use of data* for guiding instructional decisions became a focal initiative in both Jefferson and Monroe.

The remainder of this chapter analyzes district efforts within each of these areas of reform in greater detail. At the end of the chapter, we illustrate how the instructional improvement efforts within and across the three districts yielded mixed results. In particular, districts made the most progress in achieving the intended intermediate outcomes in the areas of curriculum guidance and data use, whereas results in the areas of instructional leadership and school-based coaching were more inconsistent.

Principals' Instructional Leadership

All three districts pursued similar actions to support principals' instructional leadership. These actions included professional development seminars, instructionally focused principals' meetings, instructionally focused supervision of principals, new or revised roles and responsibilities for principals, new district-based preparation programs for principals, and support for principals to attend IFL meetings in Pittsburgh. In general, the three study districts each focused their actions on principals' professional development and supervision. Other actions related to promoting instructional leadership were carried out to a lesser degree—or less consistently—across districts.

Consistent Emphasis on Professional Development and Supervision of Principals

All three districts placed a great deal of emphasis and investment in principal professional development—providing the equivalent of at least one all-day professional development seminar per month. The IFL played a major role in these efforts in all three districts, which generally included codesigning and delivering monthly all-day or half-day seminars over the course of three or four years. The IFL training focused primarily on increasing principals' knowledge of standards and instruction and how to provide support and accountability for instructional improvement. Although some districts also provided principals with non-IFL led professional development, the IFL played an important role in helping all three districts design and deliver instructional leadership training.

All three districts also attempted to build supervisory relationships that emphasized instruction. For example, in both Monroe and Roosevelt, district leaders reorganized the district structure in the past several years to include level supervisors[1] (i.e., supervisors of elementary, middle, and high schools) so that supervisors could provide support and expertise that was particular to those grade levels. In all three districts, supervisors of principals were expected not only to lead professional development and administrative meetings with their principals but also to regularly visit principals' schools to observe, provide

---

[1] We use the term *supervisor* to represent central office staff administrators who manage, support, and formally evaluate principals. The official job titles for such supervisor positions vary by district (e.g., assistant superintendent, area superintendent, director). We used this terminology in all interview and survey instruments.

feedback, support, and hold principals accountable for improving instruction and student performance in their schools.

The individual supervisors in each district, however, varied in the extent to which they were able to carry out these responsibilities—for a number of reasons. First and foremost, the amount of time supervisors could spend in individual schools depended on the number of schools within their jurisdiction and the extent to which their roles and responsibilities included other programs and initiatives. Principals also reported that individual supervisors had different past experiences (e.g., more or less experience as instructional leaders in schools) and therefore not only approached the supervisory role in different ways but also encouraged principals to prioritize different aspects of their roles. Thus, the extent to which individual supervisors emphasized instructional leadership varied within districts.

To some degree, all the districts attempted to revise or reinforce instructional leadership roles and responsibilities of principals. The three districts took slightly different approaches—for example, Roosevelt revised its formal job descriptions for principals that it used during the recruiting and hiring process, whereas Monroe reinforced instructional leadership practices by distributing a list of "clear expectations" for principals. While these formal declarations of principals' roles and responsibilities legitimized instructional leadership practices, they were reportedly not as influential in fostering instructional leadership as the professional development and supervisory strategies just discussed. This is not surprising given that districts invested a great deal more time and resources in professional development activities than in revising and reinforcing principals' roles and responsibilities.

Finally, Roosevelt and Jefferson developed and implemented new preparation programs designed to develop a pool of incoming principals with the appropriate training and skills, including instructional leadership skills. In fact, the aspiring principals program in Roosevelt was codeveloped and led by the IFL during its first year and focused almost exclusively on instructional leadership skills. The Jefferson program and the second year of the Roosevelt program were substantively broader, but served as an important strategy within the districts' larger efforts aimed at instructional leadership because both districts had had significant turnover in principals.

Greater Alignment of District Actions in Monroe and Roosevelt

District actions in the area of instructional leadership were more aligned with each other within Monroe and Roosevelt than in Jefferson. Principals in Monroe and Roosevelt reported receiving clear and consistent messages from the district regarding how to prioritize their roles and responsibilities. In these two districts, principals' supervisors were typically involved in designing professional development seminars and other district meetings for principals; they therefore reinforced the messages presented in those meetings. Monroe further emphasized coherence and consistency by explicitly articulating to principals how the various meetings and professional development opportunities were intended to support multiple principal needs and district expectations. In Jefferson, on the other hand, principals and district leaders acknowledged that the district frequently sent principals conflicting messages about the priority of spending time on instructional leadership tasks. Although the district communicated the expectation that principals should focus on instruction, it also gave priority to an increasing number of management responsibilities that constrained principals' time to work on instructional matters.

Principals Varied in Degree of Reported Instructional Leadership Actions

Principals across the three sites varied greatly in the degree to which they were acting as instructional leaders. In particular, variation existed in the degree to which principals used specific practices identified in previous studies of effective instructional leaders, such as being knowledgeable about teaching and learning, being able to skillfully observe instruction and provide valuable feedback, creating schoolwide dialogues around models of quality student work, setting goals for instructional improvement, assessing progress, identifying professional development needs, and emphasizing success for all students by placing particular emphasis on improving instruction for poorly performing students (Blase and Blase, 1999; Gates, Ross, and Brewer, 2000).

Across the three districts, most principals were at a minimum carrying out basic aspects of instructional leadership by emphasizing the importance of instructional improvement and arranging for teacher support to achieve that improvement. For example, in all three districts, more than two-thirds of teacher survey respondents reported that their principals had given them useful feedback and/or suggestions on their teaching at least a few times since the beginning of the year. Teachers were also consistent in noting that their principals emphasized instruction. As displayed in Table 4.1, the vast majority of teacher survey respondents across districts reported that their principals set high standards for teaching and learning. Many case study teachers supported this further by reporting that their principals consistently tied instructional activities to improvement in student performance in faculty meetings, professional development, and other communications with teachers. In addition, 60 to 70 percent of teacher survey respondents across districts reported that their principals arranged for support (such as access to coaches, outside consultants, and district curriculum staff) when they needed it.

At the same time, some noteworthy differences also existed between districts in the extent to which principals implemented specific instructional leadership practices. For example, as Table 4.2 illustrates, more than half of principal survey respondents in Monroe and Jefferson—compared with only a third in Roosevelt—reported that

Table 4.1
Percentage of Teachers Agreeing or Strongly Agreeing About Support Provided by Their Principals

	Monroe	Roosevelt	Jefferson
The principal at my school . . .			
Sets high standards for teaching and learning	91	80	90
Arranges for support when I need it (e.g., access to coaches, outside consultants, district curriculum staff)	68	60	69

Table 4.2
Percentage of Principals Reporting Time Spent on and Value of Reviewing Student Achievement Data

	Monroe	Roosevelt	Jefferson
How much time do you spend in a typical week reviewing student achievement data?			
Moderate to a lot of time (5–15 hours)	59	33	55
How important is reviewing student achievement data for being an effective school leader?			
Moderately to very important	98	100	97

they spent a moderate to a lot of time reviewing student achievement data. This difference existed despite the fact that nearly all the principals across the three districts similarly reported that reviewing student achievement data was moderately to very important for being an effective school leader.[2]

Factors Affecting District Efforts to Support Principals' Instructional Leadership

Several factors appeared to influence the impact of districts' efforts to foster instructional leadership among their school principals. Instructional leadership was enabled by high-quality professional development for principals as well as supportive organizational structures and supervisors. Instructional leadership was hindered by tension between instructional and managerial responsibilities, lack of perceived principal legitimacy regarding instruction, and insufficient time. Taken together, these factors suggest that enacting instructional leadership practices requires attention to issues beyond investment in professional development for principals. Institutional structures, norms, and processes are also important factors contributing to implementation of instructional leadership practices.

The ongoing, job-embedded, and tailored nature of professional development for principals promoted instructional leadership. In all three districts, several case study principals reported that

---

[2] See data use section in this chapter for a description of challenges of data use in Roosevelt.

the ongoing and job-embedded nature of professional development provided by the IFL enabled them to become more knowledgeable about instruction and how to support improvement in their school—a finding supported by national associations such as the National Staff Development Council (2000) and the Educational Research Service (1999), which encourage professional development for principals that is long-term and embedded in daily practice. For example, principals in Roosevelt reported that the IFL training was the first sustained professional development program that they had been offered by the district. Prior to the IFL partnership, principals received support through attending conferences and external professional development programs, but these opportunities were optional and "one-shot" in nature with little to no follow-up.

All three districts supplemented this core professional development with programs for aspiring principals, additional professional development sessions from non-IFL consultants, and professional development led by principals' supervisors. In addition, Monroe principals appreciated that their professional development took several different forms, such as districtwide meetings, school-level meetings, and small study groups. These multiple formats allowed principals to participate in professional development that was relevant to their individual needs, interests, and experience.

Alignment of organizational structures and supervisors facilitated support for principals. In Monroe, the reorganization of supervision of schools by level (elementary, middle, and high) allowed supervisors to develop more-focused knowledge and expertise about instruction at their assigned level. As a result, most case study principals reported that supervisors were better able to support them. In Roosevelt, a similar reorganization resulted in new supervisory positions, which allowed supervisors to devote more time to supporting principals and to prioritize this responsibility—as opposed to the previous organizational structure in which the director of special education, for example, was assigned to supervise principals in addition to the multiple responsibilities of overseeing special education programs. This may have contributed to strong positive reports about supervisors in Monroe and Roosevelt, where nearly all principals responding to the survey (95 and 93 percent, respectively) agreed that their supervisors were knowledgeable about education at their school's level.

Tension between instructional and managerial responsibilities limited instructional leadership actions. Although principals in all three districts believed instructional leadership practices were important to being an effective school leader, they also described the importance of the managerial aspects of their job, emphasizing that administrative and disciplinary issues needed to be addressed to enable effective instruction to occur. As one principal from Jefferson put it, "I'm ready to take over the charge [of instructional leadership] but somebody still needs to deal with the parent who comes in and who's upset about this, that, and the next thing." As a result, the degree to which principals were able to carry out instructional leadership tasks depended in part on the extent to which they were able to deal with managerial issues first. While instructional leadership was clearly emphasized in all three districts, individual supervisors varied in the guidance they provided to principals on how to balance new instructional leadership responsibilities with the realistic need to attend to managerial responsibilities. In interviews, principals and supervisors who described instructional leadership practices as a top priority were more likely to say they engaged in those practices on a regular basis. Further, principals who reported that they were able to balance the managerial aspects of their job also reported engaging in instructional leadership activities more frequently.

Lack of perceived principal legitimacy regarding instruction limited effective instructional leadership. Research documents that principals' efforts to become instructional leaders can be hindered by lack of credibility and/or lack of knowledge and ability (Buchen, 2002). In case study schools where teachers reported that principals were not acting as instructional leaders, teacher respondents typically did not consider their principal to be knowledgeable about instruction or an appropriate source of support for instructional matters. One explanation provided by teachers was the lack of experience teaching core academic subjects on the part of some principals. For example, one elementary school teacher explained, "Our principal is a former music teacher so I don't think he quite understands regular classrooms . . . . We're at a disadvantage because he doesn't understand a lot of the curriculum." In addition, at the secondary level, particularly in high schools, teachers explained that they believed themselves to be experts in their subject area and therefore considered it inappropriate for the principal to provide guidance on how to improve instruction. For example, when asked whether the principal was supportive on instructional matters, one high school teacher from Jefferson said, "I wouldn't think of bothering her [regarding instructional issues]. We teach, she manages the building, it is a cooperative partnership." Another high school teacher from Roosevelt similarly responded, "I should be the expert." District leaders were well aware of this issue. As one explained, "It's not easy because the principals are reinforced by the faculty to the extent they stay focused on management issues. When they move over to instructional issues, the faculty is not as happy with them because faculties traditionally don't want a lot of, as they would say, interference in the classrooms."

Insufficient time restricted instructional leadership activities. Principals in all three districts struggled to find time to carry out instructional leadership tasks given other managerial and student discipline–related responsibilities. This finding supports previous research that suggests lack of time can be an obstacle to principals becoming effective instructional leaders (Buchen, 2002). More than half of teacher survey respondents in each district reported that their principal had little time to regularly visit classrooms. In Jefferson, lack of time was particularly problematic because the district was reportedly overburdening principals with reports, requests, and compliance demands that resulted in limited opportunities for principals to be in classrooms. As one elementary school principal explained:

> I know the district is really pushing to help us to become instructional leaders but it doesn't seem like they ever take anything off our plate so that we can do that. It just doesn't seem like it ever gets done. There's always a new form that has to be filled out or a survey that we have to do, state regulation that we have to comply with and we really spend a lot of our time doing those kinds of things. I'd like to spend more time in the class-

room, I make efforts to do that, but sometimes you just get dragged away to meetings, dragged away to do other things.

The majority of case study principals in schools with large enrollments, such as middle and high schools, suggested that the size of their school limited their ability to act as instructional leaders because they had larger numbers of classrooms to visit and more teachers to support. One high school principal from Jefferson rhetorically asked, "In such a large building with management demands, how can the administration really be aware of and monitor teacher instruction?"

IFL's Role in Supporting Instructional Leadership Was Consistent and Strong

District leaders and principals in all three districts pointed to the IFL as a major support for their instructional leadership efforts. First and foremost, the IFL emphasized the importance of principal professional development based on its previous association with New York Community District 2, where instructional leadership by principals had been a primary focus. In all three districts, the initial partnerships included the IFL designing or codesigning and delivering monthly principal professional development sessions. These sessions resulted in a great deal of investment in principals' knowledge about instruction. As one Jefferson district leader described the IFL's impact on the district's instructional leadership efforts, "The IFL . . . brought us to a different level involving principals and instructional leaders. Just totally a different level. Showing us that principals needed certain skills of what to look at and how to look at their building in different ways."

In addition to directly providing professional development to principals, the IFL also encouraged and trained district administrators to become instructional leaders and to emphasize instructional improvement throughout the system. As part of its work with district administrators, the IFL influenced district leaders' understanding of what it means to be an instructional leader, such as the importance of spending time in classrooms and the importance of giving principals and teachers opportunities for learning. In at least two of the districts, district administrators reported that the IFL encouraged them to lead meetings for principals that were more focused on teaching and learning as opposed to the previous operational or administrative topics, thereby making regular district meetings a source of professional development for principals.

Over the course of the partnerships, the IFL provided both principals and district leaders with tools and resources, such as Learning Walk protocols, to support instructional leadership. When invited, the IFL also assisted districts with other efforts to support instructional leadership, such as providing training in the aspiring principals programs and consulting district leaders in revising formal roles and responsibilities of principals. As a result of the IFL's various forms of support, both district and school leaders reported that they became more knowledgeable about instruction and were better able to observe, comment on, and support instructional improvement. (See Chapter Six for further discussion.)

School-Based Coaches to Support the Professional Learning of Teachers

In two of the study districts, Roosevelt and Jefferson, significant investments were made in school-based instructional specialists, or coaches, as a method of providing teacher support and professional development and as a strategy for furthering the implementation of other districtwide instructional initiatives. Both districts secured a multi-year funding source to support the coaching position, worked to define the coaching role, recruited and hired coaches from within the district, partnered with external organizations such as the IFL to advise and/or provide training to coaches, provided professional development for coaches, redefined teacher professional development in light of the presence of school-based coaches, and negotiated with the teachers' union to ensure acceptance of coaches.

Beginning in the 2000–01 school year in Roosevelt and 2003–04 school year in Jefferson, site-based coaches were in place in the majority of schools. Both districts placed full-time

English–language arts coaches in all schools; math coaches were placed in a more limited fashion. In Roosevelt, full-time math coaches were placed only at the elementary level, while in Jefferson full-time math coaches were placed in schools identified for improvement. All other Jefferson schools received a part-time math coach.

Districts Implemented Different Coaching Models: Curriculum- Versus School-Centered Approaches

Although both Jefferson and Roosevelt had similar, overarching goals related to school-based coaching—to build the instructional capacity of schools by providing support and training to teachers and to assist with the implementation of other instructional initiatives—the specific nature and focus of coaches' work varied across the districts. First, the focus of coaches' work was more district-driven and standardized across schools in Roosevelt than in Jefferson. In Roosevelt, the coaching model was more curriculum-centered—that is, coaches' primary role was to provide professional development to teachers to advance the implementation of districtwide curriculum components. Coaches, along with district-based coaching coordinators, organized and delivered professional development that was dictated by the district and focused primarily on the curriculum programs at each grade level. Coaches used common planning time, to the extent that it was available on a school-by-school basis, and districtwide professional development days to deliver content to teachers. Although district leaders intended coaches to work individually with a subset of teachers in their school, this aspect of the coaching role was perceived by coaches to be of lower priority and often did not take place consistently. As a result, coaches generally served as turnkeys for conveying district messages regarding curriculum to teachers. As one coach said when describing her role, "The first priority would be to carry out what the district has hired me to do, which is making sure that people are doing the curriculum."

In contrast, coaches' work in Jefferson was driven by the school improvement plan (SIP) at each school and therefore was more school-centered. Although the SIP process itself followed a district-mandated and standardized format, the process resulted in each school having identified a school-specific set of weaknesses in student performance, goals to attain to address each area of weakness, and strategies to address each goal. The coaching role was developed with the intention of assisting schools in the implementation of their SIPs by providing timely, on-site professional development for teachers based on the school's individual needs. Coaches' work included modeling lessons, working with individual teachers or groups of teachers, planning and presenting professional development to faculty members, administering student assessments, helping teachers analyze student assessment data, and assisting with the implementation of district curriculum and state standards.

Coaching Role Valued in General, Yet Teachers Reported Strong Preferences for Individualized Interactions

In general, teachers in both districts who had coaches available to them reported strong, positive perceptions about their coaches' knowledge and about the value of interacting with their coaches. As Table 4.3 illustrates, for both literacy and math coaches, approximately three-fourths or more of teachers responding to the survey felt coaches were knowledgeable about content and pedagogy and more than two-thirds thought of their coaches as people they could trust to provide support when needed. A large percentage of teachers with a coach available also reported having worked with their coaches individually on a regular basis, with 45 percent and 40 percent of teachers in Jefferson and 51 percent and 50 percent of teachers in Roosevelt reporting having worked with a literacy or math coach, respectively. Teachers further reported positive opinions of their work with coaches. For example, more than half of teachers reported that the feedback and/or suggestions about their teaching given by their coaches were useful, while around half of teachers felt their coaches had helped them make important changes to their instructional practice.

Table 4.3
Percentage of Teachers Agreeing or Strongly Agreeing About Support Provided by Coaches

	Literacy Coach		Math Coach	
	Roosevelt	Jefferson	Roosevelt	Jefferson
My coach . . .				
Is knowledgeable about content and pedagogy in his/her area of assignment.	81	87	74	82
Is someone I trust to help me and provide support when I need it.	73	76	68	74
Has worked with me individually on a regular basis.	51	45	50	40
Has given me useful feedback and/or suggestions about my teaching.	68	67	64	60
Has helped me to make important changes to my instructional practice.	57	51	56	47

NOTES: The table reports the percentage of teachers with coaches available reporting that they received various support from their literacy and/or math coach(es). Teachers who did not have a coach available to them in the given subject area did not respond to this set of questions.

Although survey results indicated teachers had positive overall perceptions of their coaches, case study interviews revealed a more nuanced set of findings—indicating that some interactions with coaches were more beneficial than others. In both districts, teachers interviewed were more likely to find value in interactions with coaches when the content of coaching sessions related to individual school and/or teacher needs and when coaching was given in the form of individual advice about instruction. These preferences may explain why case study teachers in Jefferson—where the coaching role was defined by school-specific needs—were more likely than their Roosevelt counterparts to describe the content of coaching sessions as relevant to their classroom and school context.

Case study teachers in Roosevelt frequently complained that standardized interactions with coaches were of limited usefulness and could have been more useful if coaches were simply present during lesson planning to respond to teachers' questions. As one teacher put it,

> [Coaches] are really supposed to be teachers that teach us, that provide support for us. Instead they get used in a way that doesn't benefit us . . . filtering through the district's mandates in a way that we're supposed to understand . . . . They're asked to present abbreviated, hurried professional development in 40 to 50 minutes once or twice a month. That's ineffectual.

Some case study coaches in Roosevelt voiced a strong preference for acting in a more teacher- or school-centered way, but reported that the required task of delivering district messages about curriculum limited their available time to do so. As one Roosevelt coach noted, "I haven't been able to get some of the PD things done that I know would help in my building . . . because I'm handed almost like a script every time and told, 'Here, do this.'" Another coach, who hoped the district would make coaching more individualized, remarked, "Let's keep focusing on the [districtwide] agenda . . . but let's make it a little more teacher-driven while still staying within that path." Thus, Roosevelt coaches experienced significant role conflict, tugged in opposing directions by teachers wanting more individualized support and district leaders wanting them to reach as many teachers as possible.

In contrast, Jefferson coaches had the latitude to target the content of their interactions to individual needs and to act in an advisory role. This form of coach-teacher interaction was more prevalent in elementary schools, where smaller faculties and the nearly uniform teaching of math and ELA across the majority of classrooms promoted a stronger, widespread role for coaches within their schools. In these schools, teachers reported that interactions with coaches had a significantly greater impact on their instructional practices. As one Jefferson teacher expressed it, "I feel wonderful when they [coaches] come into my group and I'm learning from them, probably more than the kids are. I welcome that they can come in and have their bag of tricks." In secondary schools, where coaches focused their attention on teachers within their discipline and where teachers were seen as subject matter experts, many coaching interactions were limited to providing technical assistance. For example, several secondary coaches described helping teachers set up and use technology carts, or providing teachers with additional physical resources (e.g., books, materials) to use in their classrooms. Though these interactions were reported as being helpful, they were less directly related to reported changes in teacher instructional practice.

Factors Affecting the Implementation of School-Based Coaches

In both districts, interactions were found to be more valuable when coaches served as advisors to teachers on school-specific and/or teacher-specific issues. The implementation of school-based coaching strategies in these two districts was also influenced by limited time for teacher-coach interactions, a lack of clarity in the definition of the coach's role, and the alignment of coaching models with other district initiatives.

Limited time for teachers to work with coaches restricted interactions and their potential impact. The need for teacher flexibility to meet with coaches and time for one-on-one meetings, in-class work, planning, and reflecting on teacher-coach interactions were all found by recent research to be important factors in the success of coaching models (Boston Plan for Excellence, 2002; Neufeld and Roper, 2003a, 2003b; Poglinco et al., 2003; Richard, 2003). Yet, in both districts, teachers' union regulations constrained the use of teachers' free time. Coaches were not able to meet with teachers during teachers' free periods or before or after school unless initiated or agreed to by teachers. Coaches were also unable to observe or participate in teachers' classrooms without being invited by teachers. Regulations such as these greatly limited coaches' access to teachers, particularly in terms of planning for one-on-one meetings, and in some cases led to sessions that were more spontaneous and unplanned and therefore often less meaningful.

Additionally, the lack of common planning time in some schools limited effective teacher-coach interactions. For example, in Jefferson, common planning time for teachers in particular grade levels or disciplines was only available in a small number of schools and was up to the discretion of individual principals and school schedules. In schools where common planning time occurred on a limited basis, teachers and coaches described the time as crucial to enabling discussion of student needs and determination of strategies to effectively address them. Where common planning time was not available, teachers and coaches were limited in their opportunities to interact.

Finally, coach time to meet with teachers was limited by the amount of time coaches spent out of the school building attending district meetings and/or training sessions. Approximately one-quarter of teachers in both districts with a coach available reported on surveys that coaches had little time to support teachers and that their coaches spent too much time out of the school building. Teachers and coaches interviewed in both districts similarly reported that teacher-coach interactions were restricted by the amount of time coaches spent out of the building. These findings echo recent research findings that ongoing training for coaches is important as long as it does not take coaches away from their schools too often (GWU, 2001).

Lack of clarity in definition of coaching role limited coaches' effectiveness. Particularly in Jefferson, a lack of clarity concerning the coaching role affected the potential effectiveness of coaches. While district leaders held a clear, general notion of the coach's role as one of supporting SIP implementation, many individuals in schools we visited believed that the district did not clearly communicate this understanding at the outset and that the role was not specified adequately to help coaches organize their daily work. Coaches reported receiving mixed messages, or no messages at all, about their responsibilities when they initially began in the role of coach. When messages were received, the large number and wide range of responsibilities given to coaches limited their time to work with teachers and created questions about where they should focus their efforts. Conflicting messages about the degree to which the district was directing coaches' work and how coaches should prioritize their time increased the confusion on the part of coaches. Research on existing coaching models further supports the idea that a lack of a clearly specified role, misunderstandings among school staff about the coaching role, and additional responsibilities for coaches can all confuse and undermine coaches' work (GWU, 2001; Neufeld and Roper, 2003b; Poglinco et al., 2003; Richard, 2003).

Alignment of coaching role with other district initiatives enabled implementation of coaching model in both districts. District actions to align the coaching role with other ongoing, focal initiatives within the district played a strong, positive role in promoting effective implementation of the coaching model. Although there was a lack of clarity early in the program about coaches' specific responsibilities in Jefferson, there was a clear notion among coaches and other school staff that in general coaches were in place to help schools further analyze student data, identify areas of weakness, and assist with implementing strategies to address identified areas of need. Therefore, while Jefferson's coaches were in a sense overwhelmed with the various tasks they were expected to perform, the fact that the range of tasks was firmly centered on school-specific improvement strategies worked to increase their overall effectiveness.

IFL's Role in Influencing School-Based Coaching Models Varied

The IFL played very different roles in affecting coaching efforts across the two districts. In Roosevelt, the IFL directly influenced the district's thinking about coaching as a model for supporting teachers' professional development and in the design and implementation of the model. IFL staff members participated in conversations about the definition of the coaching role and provided training to elementary literacy coaches using the IFL's CFC model. The IFL played a more indirect role in influencing Jefferson's coaching model. District leaders credited the IFL with showing them that school-based coaching positions may be an effective model for supporting teacher professional development and building school-level instructional capacity, but there was less evidence to suggest that the IFL helped them design their coaching model (e.g., the definition of coaches' responsibilities, the training program for coaches). Although district members from Jefferson had knowledge of the IFL's coaching model and this probably influenced district thinking to some degree, a direct impact was less evident. The IFL did play a small role in the implementation of the coaching model in Jefferson by providing a few training sessions to coaches.

Curriculum Specification

In the face of increasing accountability pressures, all three districts invested in specifying curriculum to assist teachers in teaching to state standards, preparing students for state tests, and bringing greater consistency of instruction across the district. Curriculum guidance involved the creation of standards-aligned documents that provided timelines and sequencing for covering required material. For example, a nine-week planning guide for fifth grade reading in Monroe identified the key knowledge and skills from state standards to be addressed, as well as suggested curricular resources, number of days to spend on the unit, student work products, and assessments. The guides also contained teaching notes and sample lesson plans.

This type of district-directed curriculum guidance was considered a cultural shift for all three districts, where schools had traditionally operated with relative autonomy and little guidance. Although similar in purpose across districts, the curriculum documents varied with respect to several important factors, including the academic subjects and grade levels covered in the guides, the degree of flexibility teachers had to modify material found in the guides, and how the curriculum guides tied into other district initiatives aimed at improving instruction. In general, the majority of teachers in all three districts reported using the guides and, to varying degrees, found them useful resources for planning instruction in their classrooms.

Curriculum Guides Were a Driving Force for Improving Instruction in Two Districts

While all three districts developed curriculum guides, district leaders in Monroe and Roosevelt viewed the guides as a major focus of their efforts to improve instruction in all schools and invested heavily in both supporting and monitoring teachers' use of the guides. In both districts, leaders developed the curriculum guides to drive reform and ensure common, equitable teaching and learning opportunities across the district. As one Monroe leader explained, "the urgency was there to ensure that all of our students had equal access to a rigorous, challenging curriculum." Similarly, another reported that prior to developing these guides:

> We didn't have agreement on the standards, we didn't have agreement on the expectations in some scope and sequence. Because then that's what drives your professional development. That's what drives your curriculum development. That's what should drive your investment of resources. And we had too much variability within schools and across schools.

The development and implementation of curriculum guides in these two districts were closely tied to other key district initiatives, including the introduction of district assessments to regularly monitor students' progress in Monroe and the use of school-based coaches to support teachers in Roosevelt.

With respect to the structure of the curriculum guidance provided by districts, both the nature of the guidance provided and the subjects and grade levels covered in the documents differed across districts. Monroe's guides were the most comprehensive, both in the range of subject areas and grade levels covered and in the consistent inclusion of sample lesson plans, suggestions for classroom assessments, and lists of available resources and additional materials in all guides.

Despite differences in the relative focus on guides and in the nature of the guides in each district, teachers and principals in each site identified curriculum guides as a key focus of their professional development activities in the most recent school year. More than 60 percent of both teacher and principal survey respondents in all three districts indicated that implementing curriculum guides and using them to guide instruction, for teachers and principals respectively, was a moderate or major focus of their professional development activities in 2003–04.

Curriculum guides in all three districts aimed to provide teachers with detailed information about what they should teach in their classrooms throughout the school year. Across districts, teachers regularly used curriculum guides and found some of the suggestions useful, but they did not report that guides influenced their pedagogical practice, or *how* they taught their lessons. In interviews, teachers reported that guides helped them stay on track for teaching state standards during the year but noted that they did not dramatically change their daily practice. For example, as one Monroe middle school teacher noted, "they're kind of like sailing a ship with a compass . . . ever so often I look at them and I check off to see that I'm basically covering all the things I need to cover. . . . I don't feel like they're the be-all and end-all." More specifically, a strong majority of teacher survey respondents in all three districts (75 percent in Monroe, 83 percent in Roosevelt, and 84 percent in Jefferson) reported that they regularly used the guides to plan their lessons, in contrast to their perceptions of the usefulness of suggestions included in the curriculum guides for various purposes (see Table 4.4). Although a majority of teacher survey respondents in all three districts agreed that the guides provided useful suggestions for assessing student progress, fewer than half of the respondents in each of the districts agreed that the guides provided useful suggestions about instructional strategies.

Curriculum Guides Useful for the System, but Challenges Existed at the Classroom Level

The key benefit of the curriculum guides, as identified by district leaders, principals, and teachers, was that they promoted consistency

Table 4.4
Percentage of Teachers Agreeing or Strongly Agreeing About Usefulness of Curriculum Guides

	Monroe	Roosevelt	Jefferson
Guides provide useful suggestions for assessing student progress (e.g., end-of-unit tests/projects)	67	52	68
Guides provide useful suggestions about instructional strategies (e.g., how to group students, how to individualize instruction)	40	30	48

in curriculum across schools. Teachers and principals interviewed in all three districts understood the rationale for having standardized guides, citing high rates of student mobility and the need to provide all students equal access to high-quality, standards-aligned instruction. They agreed that the increased consistency of instruction across schools helped ensure that teachers at different schools taught the same material in the same order, thus easing student transfers between schools. Additionally, curriculum guides paved the way for increased continuity between grades, both within and across schools. The perceived need for grade-to-grade curricular alignment is consistent with several studies that have shown that students have greater motivation to learn when their curricular experiences are connected to and build on each other (Bransford, Brown, and Cocking, 1999; Greeno, Collins, and Resnick, 1996; Mayer and Wittrock, 1996; Newmann, 1981; Pittman, 1998). Nearly three-fourths of all teacher survey respondents and more than 95 percent of principal survey respondents in all districts agreed that guides promoted consistency of instruction among classes at the same grade level as well as continuity of instruction between grades.

Not only did administrators strongly agree with the guides' ability to increase consistency and continuity across classes and schools; they also found the curriculum guides useful for monitoring teachers' instruction. Principals in all three districts noted that the guides helped them know what teachers should be teaching at a certain point in the school year. More than 80 percent of principal survey respondents in each district reported that curriculum guides helped them better observe and give feedback to teachers.

Despite the clearly articulated benefits of the curriculum guides, principals and teachers highlighted problems with respect to the guides' pacing and ability to address the needs of all students. Teachers in all three districts indicated that the guides had unrealistic pacing timelines and, on the survey, a strong majority of teachers agreed that the guides included more content than could be adequately covered in a year (75 percent in Monroe, 67 percent in Roosevelt, and 72 percent in Jefferson). Teachers also expressed concern that the guides did not address the needs of all students. Approximately 70 percent or more of teacher survey respondents in each district disagreed or strongly disagreed that the guides appropriately addressed the needs of special student populations, including LEP students and students with individualized education plans.

Factors Affecting Implementation and Perceived Usefulness of Curriculum Guides

Overall, teachers and principals found curriculum guides useful for planning and monitoring instruction. However, several factors influenced the degree to which curriculum guides were used in classrooms. District monitoring practices, staff capacity to oversee a thorough development process with teacher input, and perceived usefulness of the guides in preparing students for state tests enabled the use of guides. In contrast, competing priorities and lack of timely delivery of documents appeared to limit their use.

Monitoring practices held principals and teachers accountable for implementing the guides. Districts' use of strategies to monitor teachers' implementation of curriculum guides has been shown to improve implementation (Snipes et al., 2002). All three districts pursued strategies for monitoring teachers' use of the guides, but these strategies differed across districts. Monroe district leaders introduced district assessments aligned with the curriculum guides, creating strong incentives for teachers to cover a set amount of material prior to the regular "benchmarking" period (usually twice a year). District and school leaders frequently used these assessment results to determine whether schools and teachers were implementing the guides and if they needed additional assistance. District leaders also provided additional curriculum support to lower-performing schools in the form of weekly training sessions, where curriculum specialists helped school leaders become familiar with upcoming curriculum units and learn strategies for implementing those units. Using a different approach, district leaders in Roosevelt specified that school-based coaches were to work regularly with teachers to support their use of the guides and used this strategy equally across all schools in the district. In both Monroe and Roosevelt, district leaders and principals participated in regular Learning Walks, which helped to ensure that teachers were in step with the guides and to determine whether teachers needed additional support. Overall, a greater degree of monitoring in both Monroe and Roosevelt may have contributed to teachers' implementation of the guides.

In contrast, monitoring practices in Jefferson did not focus explicitly on curriculum guide implementation. Jefferson principals used the guides to ensure that teachers were on track, but Jefferson teachers generally had more flexibility in their daily planning. This may explain why teachers in Jefferson expressed fewer frustrations and complaints about the guides. Although almost half of all teacher survey respondents in Monroe and Roosevelt agreed or strongly agreed that the guides were too inflexible for them to effectively teach their students, only about one-fourth of teacher respondents in Jefferson agreed that this was the case.[3]

Central office capacity influenced buy-in for guides and their perceived usefulness. Monroe's district-level capacity, particularly in terms of the number of people available to oversee the development of the documents in all grades and subjects, enabled a thorough process that involved significant teacher input. District leaders reported that more than 650 teachers helped to write the documents and hundreds more helped with revisions. As a result, the guides were described by district leaders as "teacher-driven." A greater proportion of teacher survey respondents in Monroe (41 percent) agreed that their feedback was incorporated into the guides during their development and revision, compared with teachers in Roosevelt (26 percent) and Jefferson (32 percent). In interviews, Monroe's teachers who participated in writing the guides clearly conveyed stronger buy-in for both the validity and perceived usefulness of the documents than did teachers in Jefferson and Roosevelt.

Usefulness of guides in preparing students for state tests was perceived to be limited. Teachers in both Roosevelt and Jefferson questioned whether the guides would adequately prepare students for

---

[3] Additionally, at least 60 percent of principal survey respondents in Monroe and Roosevelt reported that teachers expressed frustrations with the guides, compared with the fewer than 40 percent of principals in Jefferson who agreed this was the case.

required state tests. Teachers interviewed in Jefferson noted occasions where the sequencing of some guides was poorly aligned with the state tests in some grades; in Roosevelt, teachers described instances where the guides did not cover all the material required on the state tests. In both districts, this lack of perceived alignment affected teacher buy-in and use.

Competing priorities constrained effective use of the guides. Teachers in Monroe and Roosevelt described a major tension between staying in step with standardized guides and meeting the developmental needs of individual students. Given the perceived lack of flexibility to modify the content or pacing of the curriculum guides, teachers in Roosevelt and Monroe felt restricted in the degree to which they could tailor instruction and reteach concepts when students needed additional assistance. For example, a Monroe elementary school teacher explained, "The biggest problem I have with the [curriculum guides] is that your planning is based on what someone else is saying you should be teaching at this point and not where your students are."

Lack of timeliness of documents led to teacher frustrations. During interviews, teachers in two of the districts indicated that guides often arrived late, giving them little time to review the documents and prepare their lessons. For example, in Monroe, bilingual education teachers frequently complained in interviews that the Spanish versions of the curriculum guides arrived late and were poorly aligned with the English documents. The late arrival of documents and frequent changes further inhibited teachers' ability to follow the timeline outlined in the guides.

IFL Role in Affecting District Curricular Reforms Varied

There is some evidence that IFL staff influenced districts' decisions to pursue curriculum guidance as a strategy for improving instruction and played a minor role in the development and monitoring of the use of guides. For example, district leaders in Monroe partially credit the IFL with their decision to focus on curriculum guidance as an instructional improvement strategy. The IFL fellow participated in informal conversations with district leaders and provided relevant research for leaders to read, encouraging the district to specify a districtwide curriculum. Similarly, IFL staff members engaged in conversations with district leaders in Roosevelt that may have helped leaders think through what math and literacy programs to adopt.

As for the implementation of curriculum guides, IFL Learning Walks were used to monitor teachers' use of the guides in at least two of the districts. In addition, curriculum guides in all three districts mentioned the Principles of Learning in various, limited ways. For example, the POLs were integrated into Monroe and Roosevelt's curriculum guides by means of brief examples throughout the documents showing how to apply POLs to various units of instruction. In Monroe, a six-week eighth grade math guide included four references to Clear Expectations and one reference to Accountable Talk. Each of these references included one or two short sentences and a Web link to an outline of all POLs, such as "Begin developing a class criteria chart with your students for 'Quality Reflections.' If you have a model of a quality reflection, share and discuss it with your students." Similarly, a six-week third grade reading guide included a text box on each page providing a one- or two-sentence "teaching tip" connected to a POL. However, curriculum guides in Jefferson did not include similar suggestions throughout the curriculum documents; instead, there was a page at the back of each document listing POLs and their definitions.

Overall, teachers and principals in all three districts reported that they were aware of the references to the POLs in their curriculum guides but questioned how meaningful these references were for affecting practice. As one Monroe principal explained,

> [T]he Principles of Learning have been inserted into the [curriculum guides], like "here's where you do Accountable Talk, here's where you do Socializing Intelligence" . . . [but] all of the Principles of Learning are meant to be more states of mind of a teacher as this year's planning and implementing of curriculum, and interacting with students. . . . And to make a procedure, I don't think it changes people's thinking that much.

We discuss the use and perceived usefulness of POLs and Learning Walks further in Chapter Five.

Data Use

The study districts invested to varying degrees in strategies promoting the use of data to guide instruction and instructional decisions. These strategies included developing interim assessments and data systems, providing professional development on how to interpret and use student test results, revamping school improvement planning processes, encouraging structured review of student work, and using Learning Walks to assess the quality of classroom instruction. Overall, these efforts were generally recognized and valued by staff in all three districts. The majority of teachers and principals surveyed and interviewed reported that they had received help with data analysis from district staff (e.g., in providing useful reports and presentations of student data) and had participated in training that emphasized some form of data use.

Strong Focus on Data in Jefferson and Monroe

Despite these overall similarities, the use of data to promote instructional improvement was much more of a focus in Jefferson and Monroe than in Roosevelt. Those two districts not only invested more time and attention into data use strategies but were more consistent in achieving intended district and school-level outcomes—most notably, how useful teachers found the data to be and how much they actually used the data for instructional decisions.

First, Jefferson and Monroe placed a greater emphasis on data analysis—particularly, analysis of test score data—in staff professional development. As Table 4.5 illustrates, Jefferson and Monroe teacher and principal survey respondents were more likely than their Roosevelt counterparts to report an emphasis on the interpretation and use of student test results in the training and support they received from their school and/or district.

Table 4.5
Percentage of Teachers and Principals Reporting Moderate to Major Emphasis on Interpreting and Using Student Test Results to Guide Instruction in Professional Development Activities

	Monroe	Roosevelt	Jefferson
Teachers	68	39	68
Principals	90	73	94

Second, staff at all levels in Jefferson and Monroe reported more extensive and frequent use of data to identify areas of weakness and to guide instructional decisions. As noted above, principals in Jefferson and Monroe were much more likely to report spending at least five hours a week reviewing student achievement data. Principals interviewed repeatedly spoke about reviewing test scores to identify student, classroom, and school deficiencies, and regularly using this information to change curriculum sequencing and target resources to students and teachers.

Similarly, teachers in those two districts were more likely to report that their principals regularly helped them with data analysis. For example, approximately three-fourths of teachers responding to surveys in Jefferson (79 percent) and Monroe (72 percent) reported that their principals helped them adapt their teaching practices according to analysis of state or district assessments, compared with 56 percent in Roosevelt. Moreover, Jefferson and Monroe teachers repeatedly reported spending time in school- or grade-level meetings or professional development sessions reviewing student assessment results and other data to group students, develop targeted interventions, and identify student weaknesses and areas that required reteaching or reinforcement. District administrators in Jefferson and Monroe also were more likely to cite examples of data-driven decisions about instruction. For example, Monroe administrators decided to stop using a particular reading program at the third grade in their lowest performing schools when local assessment results showed misalignment with the state test. In addition, both districts often deployed district staff to support schools when assessment results revealed significant problems.

Finally, teachers in Jefferson and Monroe were more likely than those in Roosevelt to find data—including state and district assessment data and systematic reviews of student work—useful for guiding instruction in their classrooms. As Table 4.6 displays, Roosevelt teachers were consistently less likely to find each source of information useful for guiding instruction in their classrooms than were teachers in the other two districts. Interestingly, the majority of principals surveyed in all three districts found all these sources of information moderately to very useful for making decisions about instructional matters at their schools.

Jefferson and Monroe shared a common focus on data, but the nature of district strategies and the types of data emphasized differed greatly. Although each utilized multiple strategies, we have chosen to

Table 4.6
Percentage of Teachers Reporting That Various Types of Data Were Moderately or Very Useful for Guiding Instruction

	Monroe	Roosevelt	Jefferson
Schoolwide student performance results on *state* test(s)	50	45	60
Your students' performance results on *state* test(s) disaggregated by student groups (e.g., grade level, classrooms, student characteristics)	60	44	63
Your students' performance results on *state* test(s) disaggregated by subtopic or skill	65	48	68
Your students' performance on *district* assessments	59[a]	48	66
Results of systematic review(s) of student work	79	62	70

NOTE: The table shows the percentage of teachers reporting that they had each type of data available *and* found it to be moderately to very useful for guiding instruction in their classrooms (i.e., calculation of these percentages excluded principals and teachers who reported not having these data available). On average, 20 percent of teachers in Monroe, 24 percent in Jefferson, and 31 percent in Roosevelt reported not having these data available.

[a]For Monroe, this figure represents an average of two separate survey items: student performance on district interim assessments (an item only included on the Monroe survey) and student performance on other district assessments.

examine two initiatives given the most attention and investment during the period of study: school improvement planning in Jefferson and interim assessments linked to data systems in Monroe.

School improvement planning was emphasized in Jefferson. While school improvement planning (SIP) as a formal process occurred in all three districts, it was a more central, supported, and valued endeavor in Jefferson. Having revised the SIP process in 2002–03, Jefferson administrators encouraged school faculties to examine state assessment results by grade level—and confirm results using other assessment data—to identify areas of needed improvement in math and ELA, and to identify a realistic, narrow set of strategies to address those needs. District administrators provided schools with a new, detailed SIP template to guide this process, gave them some limited training on how to use it, and expected school coaches to assist with data analysis and implementation of the plans. The SIP process was supported even more in the 20 lowest-performing schools, where district leaders conducted periodic "SIP Implementation Visits" as well as informal visits to support and monitor SIP implementation.

As a result of the district's targeted investment in this area, school-level staff in Jefferson were more likely than their counterparts in the other two districts to identify SIP as a districtwide reform priority and focus of professional development. Moreover, teachers in Jefferson conveyed a stronger awareness of the contents of their school's plan. For example, 45 percent of teacher survey respondents in Jefferson reported that they had read their school's SIP and had a thorough understanding of it, while only 23 percent of Roosevelt teachers and 30 percent of Monroe teachers reported the same level of awareness.

Most important, school staff in Jefferson consistently described school improvement planning as useful, although labor-intensive. In interviews, principals and teachers described the process as one that helped them identify school and classroom needs. They also valued the process because it allowed for the collective identification of school goals and drew on in-house expertise. They described the plans as more meaningful than plans developed in the past and described the new SIPs as documents that truly guided their work. This contrasted with interviews in Monroe and Roosevelt, in which SIP plans were more often characterized as "compliance documents."

Teachers in Jefferson were particularly positive about the impact of the SIP on instruction. On surveys, 62 percent of Jefferson teachers reported that the SIP had influenced their teaching practice, compared with only 35 percent and 36 percent in Roosevelt and Monroe, respectively. In interviews, teachers often noted that the SIP process helped them identify, with their colleagues, ways to address student weaknesses—such as by mapping areas of weakness to curriculum to review pacing, coverage, and instructional strategies associated with each curricular unit. One middle school teacher explained that during the SIP process "we look at why students were particularly weak in a particular area and we've brainstormed and discussed what we could do in the classrooms, what we specifically do as far as teaching to address that and to improve that. So it drives instruction." Nevertheless, Jefferson teachers and principals also widely noted that the process itself was very time-consuming and challenging. For example, 78 percent of principals reported that the SIP process was more labor-intensive than it needed to be.

Interim assessments linked to data systems in Monroe. While all three districts regularly administered formative assessments, only Monroe administered a comprehensive set of standards-aligned assessments in all grades and core subjects linked to a sophisticated data management system. Leaders designed the system to provide an "early warning system on progress being made" at meeting state standards. In addition to other district-developed, formative assessments designed to measure what had been taught (e.g., "six-week tests" or "Friday assessments" that gauged what students learned during the past curricular unit or week), these interim assessments were administered at the beginning, middle, and—if there was not a state test in that subject—end of the year to assess what students knew in relation to the state standards and what they needed to know to pass the state test. As such, some administrators described them as something between formative and accountability data. Monroe leaders purchased the data system to provide quick access to results, to facilitate detailed analysis of data, and to allow for the development of additional assessments customized to a particular class, group, or student.

The results of this new initiative were positive at the administrative level in Monroe. The majority of principals and district staff interviewed found interim assessment data valid and useful and reported regularly using the system and its information for a variety of decisions, such as identifying students, teachers, and schools needing additional support (e.g., training, visits from curriculum specialists) and deciding how to design this support. More than two-thirds of principal survey respondents reported that these assessments were a good measure of student progress, and 81 percent found data moderately to very useful for making instructionally related decisions.

Teachers, however, were more mixed in their responses. Of those teachers who reported having these interim assessment data available, 59 percent found them moderately to very useful for guiding instruction in their classroom. Many teachers interviewed described looking at item analyses to break down student needs by objective, to identify topics that required reteaching and new ways of teaching, and to identify and talk with colleagues who succeeded in teaching a particular objective. The following statements from teachers in two elementary schools were typical of comments made by teachers in schools visited across the district:

> We can see which kids are low and in which . . . areas and we can decide just looking at [interim assessment results on the database] which areas we need to focus on in our class. So if my kids scored a 15 percent on facts and opinions, I know that I really need to teach facts and opinions.

> In fact one of the things we did was [for instance] if Kristen had the highest score in word meaning we'd say "okay Kristen, what are you doing in your classroom specifically in word meaning?". . . . Nadia had the highest score in summarization . . . . what specific instructions were they doing that we all thought we were actually doing but [we may have left out] one or two little components so we said, "okay then that's what we're all going to try and hit on."

Nevertheless, 60 percent of teacher survey respondents also reported that other classroom assessments provided more-useful information for planning. Many noted that classroom assessments were more thorough and provided more-timely information, or that district assessments simply duplicated what they already knew from classroom assessments and reviews of student work. As such, teachers at all levels of schooling questioned the added value of the district assessment data. For example, one elementary school teacher said,

> On [an interim assessment] . . . they may have only one question on fractions and [my students] fail that question on fractions, then all of a sudden the district says "oh they need help in fractions." But it was one question. So I feel like for me, my personal assessment—my daily anecdotal [information], the classroom teacher checks that I do, the unit test that I do—is much more indicative of where my kids are.

Similarly, a high school teacher described interim assessments as a "waste of instructional time" because "They didn't take [the interim assessment] seriously . . . and, as a certified teacher, I'm giving tests every unit, I know how my kids do. I know where their weaknesses are. I know what they've learned and what they haven't learned." Many teachers were also concerned about too much testing and time taken away from instruction and lack of time to fully utilize the data system (we heard these complaints in 14 of the 17 schools visited).

Factors Affecting Data Use

In summary, the investment in, perceived usefulness of, and use of data were stronger in Jefferson and Monroe than in Roosevelt. Although district leaders utilized different strategies, both districts created data-driven cultures. Several factors influenced districts' efforts to use data for instructional improvement purposes, including the history of state accountability incentives, access and timeliness of data, perceived validity of data, and staff capacity and support.

History of state accountability provided incentives for some to use data. The No Child Left Behind Act has created strong incentives for districts around the country to examine student achievement data and gauge student and school progress at meeting standards. Yet, unlike Roosevelt, Monroe and Jefferson experienced added pressures from long-standing state accountability systems aimed at developing individual school and student measures of achievement. Thus, these two districts had operated for years in an environment with strong incentives to carefully analyze student learning and test scores at individual student and classroom levels, which may have contributed to a stronger motivation and capacity to analyze data in this way.

Accessibility and timeliness of data limited use across and within districts. In all three districts, access to and timeliness of receiving data greatly influenced individual use. Compared with the other two districts, Monroe achieved stronger access through its online data system. Even though technological problems limited access on some campuses, most schools had the ability, on site, to see a variety of student data, disaggregate them, run item analyses, and display results in multiple formats. In contrast, school staff in Roosevelt had to issue data requests to a district administrator or an outside organization that would run the analysis for them. Roosevelt leaders recognized that this arrangement limited opportunities for data to inform decisions in a timely way and were in the process of developing an online data system. Despite these overall differences, individuals in all three districts commonly complained that data were not timely. In Jefferson, for example, principals and teachers in more than half of the schools visited criticized the district's emphasis on using state test results in the SIP process because they felt these data were out of date and less relevant than other, interim assessment data.

Perceived validity of data greatly affected data buy-in and use. School staff in each site often questioned the accuracy and validity of measures. These doubts greatly affected individual buy-in for the various data sources, which past research has identified as an important factor affecting meaningful data use (Feldman and Tung, 2001; Herman and Gribbons, 2001; Ingram, Louis, and Schroeder, 2004). In Monroe, some principals and many teachers across the case study schools questioned the validity and reliability of the interim assessments, believing that some tests had changed in quality from the first administration to the second or that students were not motivated to perform well on them. In fact, only 45 percent of teacher survey respondents felt that these local assessments were a good measure of students' progress toward mastering standards—compared with 66 percent of principals. As one high school teacher noted, "It gives downtown statistics, but the statistics are not valid." Principals and teachers in Jefferson and Roosevelt voiced similar concerns about state test data, believing the results did not provide student-level or classroom-level item analysis (in Roosevelt) or were not good measures of student skills (in Jefferson). Similar to their Monroe counterparts, many expressed a preference for classroom assessments and reviews of student work, which were seen as more meaningful and valid. As a result, to varying degrees, teachers in all three districts often reported relying on other data to inform their practice.

Staff capacity and support enabled data use. Numerous studies have found that school personnel often lack adequate capacity to formulate questions, select indicators, interpret results, and develop solutions (Choppin, 2002; Feldman and Tung, 2001; Mason, 2002). Our study districts are no exception. While we observed a range of data-use skills and expertise in all three districts, capacity gaps were most visible in Roosevelt. Compared with the other two districts, Roosevelt teachers reported feeling less prepared to use data. For example, only 23 percent reported feeling moderately to very prepared to interpret and use reports of student test results, compared with 43 percent in Monroe and 36 percent in Jefferson. Compounding the reported lack of capacity were reports that principals were less likely to help teachers with these tasks and that professional development was less focused on data use, as reported above (see Table 4.5 and the preceding paragraph). According to interviews of district leaders in Roosevelt, data use had been less of a priority for professional development because appropriate data and data systems were not yet available.

In contrast, Monroe and Jefferson made stronger district-level investments in supporting school staff with data analysis. They employed several individuals in the district office with strong data analysis skills and tasked individuals to "filter" data and make them more usable for school staff (a strategy found to be successful in several studies, such as Berhardt, 2003; Choppin, 2002; Herman and Gribbons, 2001). In Jefferson, school-based coaches often took the first step of analyzing test results and presenting them in usable forms to school faculties. Both districts also targeted the lowest-performing schools for extra support on using data, frequently presenting state and district assessment data in easy-to-read reports (Monroe) and visiting schools to assist in planning and benchmarking progress (Jefferson).

IFL Role in District Use of Data to Inform Instruction Was Limited

According to district leaders in all three districts, the IFL did not substantially influence their decision to focus on data analysis or their design of most data-use strategies. The IFL did, however, promote the implementation of one data strategy—the use of Learning Walks to assess the quality of instruction in classrooms and schools. Interview and survey data indicate that Learning Walks took place, to varying degrees, in all three districts, although more frequently in Monroe and Roosevelt. The IFL also provided protocols (e.g., the *Learning Walk Sourcebook*), tools (e.g., rubrics), and professional development for staff on how to conduct these walks, how to record observations, analyze the evidence gathered, and make judgments about the quality of instruction as it related to the Principles of Learning. As one Jefferson administrator explained, the IFL "has given us that structure" for how a group of people walk through a school, collect information, and talk about teaching. (See Chapter Six for further discussion of Learning Walks.)

Summary

Over the course of this study, the three districts implemented multiple districtwide strategies to promote instructional improvement across all schools. While making some level of investment in each area of reform—instructional leadership, school-based coaching, curriculum specification, and use of data—each district chose to place greater relative emphasis on their work within a smaller number of focal initiatives:

- **Instructional Leadership.** Each district placed moderate emphasis on promoting the instructional leadership of principals. Though not considered a focal initiative in any district during the time of this study, each district nonetheless implemented multiple strategies to support principals as instructional leaders—in particular, professional development for principals and instructionally focused supervision.
- **School-Based Coaching.** Two study districts made great investments in school-based coaching models. Math and ELA coaches were placed in the majority of schools as a method of providing teacher support and professional development, building the instructional capacity of schools, and furthering the implementation of other district initiatives. Although the districts had similar reasons for implementing school-based coaching, the coaching models differed in the nature of teacher-coach interactions and the degree to which the coaches' work was curriculum- or school-centered.
- **Curriculum Specification.** All three districts developed district-wide curriculum guidance documents, although materials varied in nature and comprehensiveness across districts. Two districts emphasized curriculum standardization as a focal reform initiative, tying curriculum efforts to other district initiatives and implementing additional strategies to monitor implementation and hold teachers and principals accountable for use of the guides.
- **Data Use.** Finally, two districts placed great emphasis on enabling data use for instructional decisionmaking at all levels of the system. Monroe achieved this goal primarily by implementing a comprehensive set of interim assessments tied to a data management system; Jefferson worked to create a data-driven culture by instituting a new, data-driven school improvement planning process.

Overall, the instructional improvement efforts within and across the three districts yielded mixed results. These results are not surprising given what we know from past research: that implementation and institutionalization of meaningful school and classroom level changes generally take more than five years to accomplish (Darling-Hammond, 1995, 1997; Hess, 1995; McLaughlin, 1991; Sizer, 1992). The area in which all three districts made the most progress in achieving the intended outcomes was curriculum guidance. In all three districts, there were reported increases in the consistency and continuity of instruction as a result of these guides. Teachers were generally using the guides regularly for planning and felt prepared to use them, and teachers and principals found them moderately useful. For the two districts that focused on data use, it too was a strong area of reform. Teachers and principals in Monroe and Jefferson generally found the various sources of data useful and reported regularly using them to identify areas of weakness and to guide instructional decisions.

Finally, outcomes associated with efforts to promote instructional leadership were inconsistent, both within and across districts. Principal survey respondents were likely to report engaging in multiple instructional leadership activities, such as providing teachers with useful feedback or suggestions on their teaching, setting high standards for teaching and learning, and arranging for teacher support when needed, whereas teachers in case study schools reported that some principals acted as strong instructional leaders but others did not. Although our data do not allow us to categorize each principal on a measure of instructional leadership, multiple data sources nonetheless show that districts have had inconsistent results in promoting instructional leadership in all schools.

What accounts for these patterns? What factors contributed to the mixed results seen in coaching and instructional leadership compared with more consistent results on data use and curricular specification? Chapters Five and Six address these questions by first examining common constraints and enablers of instructional reform in the three districts, and then describing the overarching impact of the IFL on the three districts and their reform efforts and the common factors affecting district-IFL partnerships.

Overarching Findings About District Instructional Improvement: Common Constraints and Enablers

What factors contributed to or hindered districts' success in bringing about the intermediate outcomes they intended for each set of reform strategies? Why were strategies more or less successful across districts? This chapter begins to address these questions by describing a set of overarching findings related to the relative success of district instructional improvement efforts. We draw on evidence presented in Chapter Four, as well as some additional survey and interview data, to arrive at the following set of cross-district themes. Looking across the three districts, we found a set of factors that appeared to enable and constrain district reform efforts:

- Comprehensiveness of reforms
- Focus on a limited number of key initiatives
- District capacity, including time, financial and physical resources, and staff
- Availability of on-site assistance
- Degree of policy alignment among initiatives
- Extent to which strategies engage multiple stakeholders
- Balance between standardization and flexibility
- Nature of local accountability policies
- Policy decisions at the state and federal levels.

A Comprehensive Set of Strategies Was Important for Addressing All Facets of Instruction

As described in detail in Chapter Four, each district invested to some degree in instructional improvement strategies within the four key areas of reform identified in this study and generally implemented multiple strategies within each area. Looking across the reform efforts in each district, it is clear that districts implemented a set of strategies that were "comprehensive" in at least three ways. First, as opposed to piecemeal efforts to add a program or slightly adjust one facet of the system, all three districts chose a comprehensive or systemic approach. This approach ensured that this set of reform strategies applied to all schools and stakeholders and targeted not only teacher professional development but also supervision, school accountability and data, curricular and instructional guidance, and leadership development. As one superintendent explained, the district achieved "interconnectedness" among the various reforms in the past few years:

> The [curriculum guides] now give you a sense of what the components are. See, it all starts to fit together as a whole, but before when you had data and no curriculum, you couldn't figure it out. No curriculum without data is no good. And how does professional development fit in? We've been . . . working on that.

Second, these strategies were comprehensive in their intent to influence all facets of instruction. For example, each district addressed the *content* of instruction by creating standards-based curriculum guides that provided teachers and principals with detailed information about what objectives, concepts, and skills to cover in each grade level and subject area. *Pedagogical practice* was also addressed, albeit lightly, in curriculum guides, as well as more deeply in teacher and principal professional development and coaching sessions focused on identifying and modeling effective instructional strategies, assessing student learning, and effectively organizing classrooms. Reforms also included new or revised *assessments* and guidance on ways to use assessment data to inform instructional decisions.

By engaging in multiple reforms that included a comprehensive view and treatment of instruction, districts seemingly acknowledged that work in only one area of instruction, or implementing only one strategy aimed at improving instruction within each area, would not be sufficient to bring about systemwide instructional change. This was particularly important because, as past research has shown, individual policies often affect different aspects of classroom instruction, and to different degrees (Spillane, 2004). In addition, the comprehensive nature of instructional reforms contributed to teachers' and principals' awareness of their district's prioritization of instructional improvement at all levels of the system.

A final dimension of comprehensiveness was a dual focus on providing direct support and resources to teachers and building the organizational infrastructure to enable teachers' work. The attempt to address organizational supports (such as revising supervisory structures and roles and increasing availability of data and data systems), along with direct support for classroom teachers (such as curriculum guides and direct training), also helped to advance the instructional reforms in the three study districts.

This dual investment and connection was perhaps strongest in Monroe, where leaders acknowledged that focusing solely on teachers' professional development in the absence of principals' professional development and improved supervision of principals would have been shortsighted. For example, district leaders viewed the horizontal reorganization of schools by elementary, middle, and high school levels (as opposed to vertical organization, in which supervisors manage a geographic cluster of schools at all levels) as an important structural complement to the more direct instructional improvement efforts involving teachers and principals. According to the superintendent, "by having a head of elementary or a head of middle or a head of high school, I really felt for the next five years, this structure will give us the power of best practices sharing and accountability." District leaders also intended an additional reorganization of central office staff and lines of authority to build the district's capacity to provide direct support to schools. "We want to be a district driven by teaching and learning," said the superintendent, "and . . . you do it by having a second empowered person who's a chief academic officer and you co-ordinate all those services under that person so that they're support-ing teaching and learning." Monroe leaders also experimented with the reallocation of human resources in a small group of low-performing schools, reassigning more experienced administrators to these schools and allowing new school leaders to restaff the schools. Nevertheless, during the course of the study, none of the districts opted for widescale changes to the hiring, compensation, and assign-ment of staff (although some leaders were beginning to consider such strategies).

Thus, all three facets of comprehensiveness—a systemic ap-proach, strategies addressing all dimensions of instruction, and a dual focus on infrastructure and direct instructional support—proved to be important facilitators of instructional change efforts.

Focus on a Limited Number of Initiatives Assisted in Implementing Reforms, but Tradeoffs Resulted

All three districts implemented a comprehensive set of reforms aimed at instructional improvement, but each chose to emphasize a smaller number of initiatives during the course of this study. Overall, focus-ing on two key areas of reform worked to support district efforts by sending clear and consistent messages about district priorities and fo-cusing district and school resources, to some degree, on a finite num-ber of priority areas. Districts were also able to leverage the work and investments made in focal areas to promote other, less emphasized areas of reform, allowing momentum to build for their overall reform efforts. For example, a focus on the area of data-driven school im-provement planning in Jefferson implicitly and explicitly included ties to district curriculum reforms—a less emphasized area—as schools necessarily considered district standards, curriculum, and as-sessments when creating and implementing their school improvement plans.

Although identifying and investing significant resources in focal areas of reform helped districts implement change, the decision to focus resulted in important tradeoffs. With limited resources to invest, strong district emphasis in some areas seemed to necessitate a reduced emphasis in other, important areas of work. For example, Monroe leaders recognized the value of coaching but, when faced with a fiscal deficit, chose to cut many of the coaching positions and program supports (e.g., districtwide coaching meetings). Instead, leaders invested their limited resources in what they viewed as higher priorities: the development of districtwide curriculum guides and assessment systems. As the district rolled out the new curriculum, however, leaders and school staff quickly recognized that teachers needed additional assistance to fully understand and apply the instructional techniques and content envisioned in the curriculum guides and utilize data to inform practice—needs that school-based coaches could have helped address. As one top-level administrator explained, "It is the missing link: having that ongoing teacher-led discussion about curriculum implementation. Principals can go so far and at some point you've got to have that link with lead teachers."

Additionally, making long-term significant investments of time and financial and human resources in one area may have limited districts' abilities to address new areas of need as they emerged. For example, if the full range of district resources was needed to maintain a focus on a given reform—such as the intense support needed to assist schools with the development and implementation of school improvement plans in Jefferson—district staff members and/or other resources may not have been available to address other school or district needs that arose. In Jefferson, district leaders focused the most intensive support around the SIP process in the 20 lowest-performing schools; yet because the definition of "low-performing" under NCLB is dynamic, with school classifications changing on an annual or biannual basis, they risked helping some schools at the expense of others that might be labeled low-performing the following year. District leaders repeatedly voiced this concern in interviews. One administrator noted,

> The other schools [not receiving intensive support because of relatively higher performance] got jealous, actually. And they

wanted to do all the stuff [low-performing schools were doing], but you know, what are you supposed to do? Now last year . . . six of my better schools went down on the [state test] and if that happens this year, I'm screwed.

Insufficient Capacity Was a Significant Obstacle to Instructional Improvement

Across all three districts, limited district capacity at all levels of the system was the most common barrier to reform. Capacity gaps that were most detrimental pertained to time, financial and physical resources, and staff. These findings are once again consistent with prior research, which has shown that various dimensions of district capacity—including the level of staffing, staff will, knowledge, and skills; time; and materials—can greatly affect district reform efforts (Burch and Spillane, 2004; Elmore and Burney, 1999; Firestone, 1989; McLaughlin, 1992; Spillane and Thompson, 1997; Togneri and Anderson, 2003; see Marsh, 2002, for detailed review).

First, *insufficient time for planning* constrained reform efforts at both the district and school levels. District leaders and staff members described having too little time in some cases to plan and roll out new initiatives, often experiencing tension between wanting to take more time to plan and implement initiatives and needing to address areas of need in a timely manner. For example, district leaders in Roosevelt acknowledged that some curriculum guides may have been rolled out prematurely and needed much revision after they had been given to teachers. But they felt strongly that some form of the curriculum guides, though imperfect, was needed in classrooms immediately and therefore they could not wait for additional revisions before presenting the new guides. However, across all districts, school staff viewed rushed implementation of new initiatives as problematic. More than 75 percent of principal survey respondents in each district reported that inadequate time to prepare before implementing new reforms was a moderate or great challenge to their efforts to improve teaching and learning at their schools.

Insufficient time to act as instructional leaders was also an obstacle to reform across the districts, as reported throughout Chapter Four. Principals in case study schools frequently named "time" as the greatest barrier to interacting with teachers concerning instruction and were often forced to spend a majority of their time on managerial issues. Similarly, limited time hindered coaches' abilities to assist teachers. Time for coaches to work with teachers in Jefferson and Roosevelt was restricted by union regulations about teacher free time, by the lack of common planning time in many schools, and by the amount of time coaches spent out of the building attending meetings and/or training. Finally, teachers interviewed in all three districts frequently reported limited time as a reason they often did not engage in analyzing data to the degree district leaders had intended.

Second, teachers and principals described a *lack and/or instability of fiscal and physical resources* as a challenge to instructional improvement efforts. Nearly two-thirds of teacher survey respondents in Jefferson and Roosevelt and almost half in Monroe cited inadequate resources (e.g., textbooks, equipment, teachers' aides) as a moderate or great challenge to improving teaching and learning in their classrooms. All three study districts also faced significant budget shortfalls over the course of the study, resulting in cuts to both personnel and programs. More than two-thirds of principal survey respondents in each district reported that instability of funding from year to year was a moderate or great challenge to improving teaching and learning in their schools. In fact, in all three districts, it was the most frequently cited challenge out of a list of ten other potential challenges, including teacher turnover, complying with accountability policies, and lack of high-quality professional development.

Finally, *limited capacity of central office staff,* in terms of available time, number of staff members, and areas of expertise, was also a constraint across the three districts—although most significantly in Roosevelt. For example, many reported that until recently, Roosevelt lacked an adequate number of individuals in the central office with content and instructional expertise. More recently, the district has made efforts to recruit additional staff in these areas, but the lack of capacity nonetheless affected efforts throughout the duration of the study. Additionally, Jefferson's efforts to create and implement data-driven school improvement plans, in particular to support SIPs in the large number of low-performing schools, required that district administrators provide intensive, ongoing support to school staff. Yet, district leaders and staff acknowledged that they did not have the full capacity to give the needed support to all schools in the district. Time and resources were prioritized for schools classified as low-performing by the state, often leaving a gap in needed support for other schools, many of which had similar concerns related to low student performance.

On-Site Assistance for Teachers and Principals Enhanced Instructional Capacity at the School Level

Although limited capacity of district office staff constrained district efforts in many ways, in some cases, skilled central office administrators enabled district work. That is, teachers and principals in all three districts often noted the high-quality support they received from district staff, particularly on instructional issues. When district administrators were able to work closely with school-level staff, the support they provided was of great value. This was particularly true of many curriculum specialists and directors. Teachers and principals who worked with these staff members described a strong, positive impact of these interactions on instructional practice. And, because most of these staff members were in nonevaluative roles, they were seen as more trustworthy and less threatening to both teachers and principals than top district leaders. As an elementary school principal in Monroe explained about working with a central office "director,"

> I mean, she knows instruction. She knows bilingual ed and I really feel that . . . if I . . . say, "okay, what can I do here?" . . . she would tell me and I wouldn't feel like . . . this is going to be threatening and it's going to be documented. . . . And she knows

elementary and she knows instruction, so I feel fortunate that she's been here.

The existence of on-site instructional expertise for teachers was also an enabler of district instructional improvement efforts. The school-based coaching models described in Chapter Four provided strong instructional support for teachers and principals and worked to advance the implementation of other district instructional reforms, in particular curriculum guides in Roosevelt and school improvement plans in Jefferson.

Strategies That Were Aligned and Mutually Supportive Facilitated Reform; Misalignment Greatly Constrained Efforts

District reform efforts were more effective at promoting intended outcomes when strategies were both aligned and mutually supportive—that is, implementation of one strategy helped further the goals of another. Misalignments hindered the potential success of reform efforts. Ensuring alignment of initiatives required considering the perspectives of individuals at all levels of the system. Most commonly, staff members or leaders at the district level designed systemic initiatives with school-level implementation in mind. But it was difficult to predict the realities of program implementation and how implementation would vary across classrooms and schools until the initiative was actually put into place. Thus, the school-level perspective was needed concerning the degree to which there were or might be challenges to implementing new programs—more specifically about how new programs aligned or conflicted with other programs.

Monroe provides an example of variation in perceptions of alignment. District leaders envisioned a seamless, aligned system of reforms: Curriculum documents would guide teachers on the content and pacing of material to be covered, and interim assessments would assist teachers in gauging student progress at learning curricular material and making instructional decisions (e.g., reteaching units or concepts that students did not score well on). However, from teachers' perspectives, there was a fundamental conflict between expectations to both teach to the content and pacing expectations set forth in the curriculum guides and expectations to inform instruction with local assessment results. Teachers questioned how they were supposed to both reteach topics in areas where assessment data indicated deficiencies and at the same time cover the next topics specified by the curriculum guides. Similar to the sentiments expressed by teachers throughout the district, one elementary school teacher explained:

> [Y]ou can go in [the interim assessment database] and . . . find out that . . . 70 percent of your kids didn't know how to identify setting but only 20 percent didn't know how to identify summaries or parts of summaries. So if we had the freedom to adjust our teaching, hypothetically a teacher would say "well my class most needs to know how to identify setting. So for the next week or two that's what I would be focusing on." But it's funny because we're being encouraged to use that data to drive our instruction and yet if setting is what my classroom needs and character traits is what her classroom needs, next week the [curriculum guide] says that we're supposed to be in there to [teach] summary. So neither of our classes are [sic] getting what they most need. . . . It's just a strangely mixed message.

As this comment suggests, this misalignment led to tension and frustration on the part of teachers who felt they were being held accountable to two conflicting expectations and ultimately negatively affected teacher buy-in to the curricular and assessment reforms. Faced with a decision about how to spend valuable classroom time, many teachers opted to follow the curriculum, leading to a less effective implementation of Monroe's reforms based on data use at the classroom level. Nevertheless, this same set of strategies was aligned from the perspective of school principals, who valued guides and data as complementary tools to help monitor the quality of classroom instruction.

In short, we found that both horizontal (within levels of the system) and vertical (across levels of the system) alignment of initiatives facilitated effective implementation of reform strategies. Districts were more successful when they designed initiatives and policies so that they advanced the goals of other initiatives and avoided conflicting messages or expectations. Additionally, making linkages among initiatives explicit aided in communicating clear and consistent messages about district priorities. Research on school districts affirms the importance of consistency and asserts that central office staff can play a critical role in creating this alignment (Snipes et al., 2002).

Districts Struggled to Design Reform Strategies That Enabled Multiple Stakeholders to Engage in Instructional Improvement

District leaders in all three districts faced significant challenges in designing reform strategies and policy tools that simultaneously addressed the needs of multiple stakeholders and involved them in the work of instructional improvement. For example, as discussed above, although principals and central office administrators in Monroe valued interim assessments and reported using them regularly because they provided information to monitor teacher and school progress, teachers found them to be less useful for guiding their daily work. This tension illustrates the difficulty of designing student assessments that serve multiple purposes of accountability and instructional guidance.

Similarly, as noted in Chapter Four, Roosevelt's stakeholder groups varied in the extent to which they embraced the curriculum-centered coaching model. Central office staff valued the coaching effort because it facilitated implementation of the district's curriculum guides and greater uniformity of content coverage and pacing across the district. The majority of principals also appreciated the new on-site assistance because it helped free up their time and strengthen instructional guidance on campus. In contrast, teachers were more resistant to the coaching reform effort because they did not think it met their needs for more customized support. Thus, as in Monroe, Roosevelt leaders faced a significant challenge in developing a coaching model that simultaneously met administrator and teacher needs.

Achieving a Balance Between Standardization and Flexibility Proved Difficult for Districts

By definition, strategies intended to affect the work of all teachers and principals across a district imply the need for some degree of standardization. Yet, all three districts in the study struggled to achieve a balance between standardizing initiatives, implementation, and support across all schools and allowing flexibility to meet school-specific needs. Research on school districts has identified this as a common tension among districts attempting reform and often finds that school-level improvement hinges on a district's ability to balance central authority and school autonomy (Elmore and Burney, 1999; Goldring and Hallinger, 1992; Massell and Goertz, 1999; Murphy and Hallinger, 1986, 1988; Togneri and Anderson, 2003).

For example, Roosevelt leaders developed a standardized model of principal training in which all principals met together monthly to receive and participate in the same content, often centered on the Principles of Learning. Although this model helped set common expectations and understandings about high-quality instruction, district leaders and principals realized over time that the training was not meeting the needs of all principals. In particular, principals requested training tailored to different levels of experience and schooling. Some principals described the first few years of professional development as "very strong" and "powerful," but after several years of exposure to the same topics, principals began to view these sessions as "a waste of time" because there was no flexibility to adjust the sessions to their various needs. At the end of the study, district leaders began to recognize the need for this flexibility:

> We have varying levels of knowledge and understanding of the work. How can we now differentiate how we're working with three-year people, two-year people, one-year people, first-year? There's an assumption that first-year people will need certain content experience that may become "old hat," so to speak, for third-year people, and third-year people are ready to push on. . . . And so I think one of the challenges in our work going

forward is how to address that so that we don't lose the momentum.

Similarly, other Roosevelt leaders noted the importance of differentiating training by level: "We want some level of differentiation between the elementary and the middle and the high school principals because their issues are so different at this point. Three years ago they weren't." In contrast, Monroe leaders recognized this tension several years ago and redesigned principals' training to provide greater flexibility—organizing monthly training sessions by level and allowing principals at the elementary level to select additional sessions aligned with their needs (e.g., groups focused on bilingual education, science, being a new administrator).

A second example of the challenge to balance standardization and flexibility involved district-mandated curriculum guides. Teachers in Monroe and Roosevelt repeatedly noted a tension between following the uniform pacing and content set forth in the curriculum guides and meeting the developmental needs of all students. In both cases, teachers perceived the guides as overly standardized, allowing little flexibility for tailoring or reteaching topics when students needed additional instruction. As reported earlier, almost half of all teacher survey respondents in Monroe and Roosevelt agreed or strongly agreed that the guides were too inflexible to allow them to teach their students effectively. In interviews, teachers in Roosevelt and Monroe, respectively, echoed these sentiments:

> We're not really thinking about the quality of instruction rather than quantity and we're skimming over the surface of everything. . . . They're [the district] wanting us to just go, go, go, go, not taking the children into account . . . the needs of the children.

> [The curriculum guide was] introduced as sort of a flexible suggestion or format, but it's becoming a much more dogmatic requirement . . . [It] almost forces teachers to kind of continue lying about where they have to be in their classroom . . . . These five kids simply can't be studying context clues [because] they can't decode. And so it's a real conflict . . . between

individualized instruction, which everybody agrees is necessary, and a standardized approach.

These perceptions led to negative attitudes about district efforts and decreased buy-in on the part of teachers. However, in both cases, district leaders described wanting teachers to have a greater degree of flexibility than teachers felt they had. Therefore, clearer communication was needed on the part of the districts about the degree of flexibility intended and considered acceptable.

Local Accountability Policies Created Incentives and Disincentives That Affected the Quality of Implementation of Reform Strategies

Across the districts, we found that formal and informal accountability policies served as both incentives and deterrents to high-quality implementation of reform strategies. In some instances, districts' efforts to hold teachers and principals accountable for carrying out certain initiatives promoted implementation. For example, in both Roosevelt and Monroe, where districts explicitly visited classrooms and checked in regularly with principals to assess teacher use of district-mandated curriculum guides, teachers reported using the guides in classroom practice and being aware that this was an expectation of the district for which they were being held accountable. In this sense, accountability mechanisms likely promoted implementation of curriculum guides by teachers. Similarly, when district and school leaders coupled Learning Walks with post-walk reflection among participating teachers and "walkers," the experience was said to genuinely influence teacher practice. For example, a Monroe teacher who was regularly visited and videotaped during Learning Walks and given the opportunity to discuss the experience with colleagues, reported that it changed the way she teaches:

> [N]ow I tell my kids why they need to learn this and then I have them tell me what they're learning and why, and so . . . it's changed my teaching style. . . . I think the accountable talk and

> the walk-throughs have helped me . . . . [T]he other day a fifth
> grade teacher came in and sat down on the carpet with [my stu-
> dents] and she was asking "well why are you learning this? What
> do you need to know this for and how's this going to help you
> in your life?" And my kids were able to answer all her questions,
> but I didn't do that before.

At the same time, however, the nature of district accountability
practices sometimes led to unintended negative consequences
whereby teachers and principals had a disincentive for making
meaningful changes to their practice. This often occurred when accountability tools were superficial or created incentives for "gaming
the system." Because these accountability tools had to be used on a
wide scale, they tended to measure easily quantifiable outcomes. For
example, the checklist-driven nature of the principal evaluation tool
implemented in Jefferson created a system whereby principals were
evaluated in such a way that hardly any principals in the case study
schools reported having meaningful interactions with their supervisors or saw the evaluation process as a source of support for their
work as instructional leaders. Despite district leaders' intentions when
revising this tool, principals did not see the evaluation as an incentive
to change or improve their practice.

Similarly, in Monroe, district leaders used interim assessments to
monitor school progress and in some cases categorize and recategorize
schools by level of performance throughout the year, providing more
support but less autonomy over schools in the lowest-performing
categories (e.g., school staff were required to attend special meetings,
follow curriculum guides more strictly, and participate in Learning
Walks more frequently). As a result, some schools were reported to
treat interim assessments like high-stakes tests. We heard reports of
schools giving students the assessments in advance for practice, letting
student retake them, and possibly cheating to avoid being reclassified
into a lower ranking. Other schools no longer administered the assessments in English to the ELL students—considered a voluntary
alternative to assessing in the native language and a valuable way to
measure progress at language acquisition—for fear that lower scores
would bring down the school ranking. By using interim assessments

as accountability tools rather than diagnostic tools to guide instruction (as they were intended), Monroe created incentives for some teachers and principals to participate in what some might call gaming to ensure better test results.

Policy Decisions at Higher Levels Influenced Policy Decisions and Actions at the District Level, Often with Unintended Consequences

Confirming past research on policy implementation (Fuhrman and Elmore, 1990; Honig, forthcoming; McLaughlin and Talbert, 1993; Odden, 1991), the instructional improvement efforts of the three districts are best understood in the context of the broader policy system. Even though district leaders designed the strategies examined in and across the four areas of reform, state and federal policies greatly shaped the enactment of these local strategies. As noted in Chapter Four, NCLB created incentives for district leaders in these three districts and nationally to examine student assessment data. Yet the added layer of a long-standing state accountability system in Monroe and Jefferson may have enabled greater use of data in these two districts than in Roosevelt. State incentives to examine test scores by student, groups of students, classrooms, and schools likely contributed to stronger motivation and capacity to analyze data in these two districts. Similarly, the development of state standards and assessments clearly influenced district decisions to produce detailed curriculum guides. The state, federal, and public pressure to improve student achievement and the potential consequences for failing to do so provided significant motivation for teachers to follow these documents and for administrators to encourage their use.

Nevertheless, the same accountability environment may have spawned local actions that detracted from the ultimate goal of improved teaching and learning more broadly. For example, as some teachers reported in all three districts, the curriculum guides and incentives to focus on the tested subjects may have narrowed what subjects teachers taught (e.g., elementary teachers gave less time or no time to social studies and art) and removed some of the depth of instruction that many believe to be critical for student learning. The creation of interim assessments—viewed by district leaders as a tool for gauging students' progress at learning to state standards and their level of preparedness for state testing—may have also had unintended consequences. For example, many teachers and principals in Monroe felt that district leaders had turned these seemingly diagnostic assessments into high-pressure, punitive measures that were undermining teacher morale and the learning environment. As one principal reported on the survey,

> The [interim] assessments should not be viewed by district administrators and curriculum specialists as diagnostic tools to rank-order and penalize campuses. The knee-jerk reactions create an environment of distrust among teachers and will jeopardize the reliability and true purpose of [interim] assessments.

Other principals and teachers repeatedly mentioned "the specter of fear" and "scare tactics" being used throughout the district with regard to the sorting of schools based on test scores, and the stigma and stress associated with labels district administrators gave to schools that fell into the lower ranks.

Summary

The factors presented in this chapter contributed to the overall progress of each district's reform efforts. Taken as a whole, these factors led to several cross-cutting findings:

- **Although it was important for districts to implement comprehensive reform, they benefited from focusing on a small number of initiatives.** While it seems counterintuitive, a combination of comprehensiveness and focus proved to be important for facilitating instructional reform in all three districts. All three facets of comprehensiveness—a systemic approach, strategies addressing all dimensions of instruction, and a dual focus on infrastructure and direct instructional support—helped target the problem of instruction from all angles. Focusing on two key areas of reform complemented these efforts by sending clear and consistent messages about district priorities and channeling limited district and school resources, to some degree, into a finite number of areas. Nevertheless, it is important to keep in mind that districts also faced significant tradeoffs by deciding to focus on certain areas of reform.

- **District and school capacity greatly affected reform efforts.** Although focusing on a few high-priority initiatives may have helped conserve limited resources to some extent, all three districts nonetheless faced significant capacity gaps—the most detrimental relating to time, fiscal resources, and district staff—that greatly hindered instructional improvement efforts. At times, however, the districts capitalized on capacity strengths, such as assistance from knowledgeable district staff and on-site instructional specialists, which enabled district reform.

- **Districts' success also was tied to several key dimensions and characteristics of the policies they developed.** District progress at achieving intermediate instructional improvement goals hinged in large part on the degree to which strategies (1) were aligned and mutually supportive, (2) enabled multiple stakeholders to engage in reform, (3) found an appropriate balance between standardization across schools and flexibility to meet school-specific needs, and (4) were enforced by local accountability policies that provided incentives for meaningful change to instructional practice. Of course, districts generally struggled to achieve these policy features, which might be better characterized as common challenges or tensions districts faced in achieving systemwide change.

- **The broader policy context created both enabling and constraining conditions for district reform.** At a local level, some union policies hindered reform in two districts, most notably by limiting the time available for teachers and coaches to work together. In addition, state and federal policies, particularly accountability policies, shaped much of the districts' work with curriculum and data use. These accountability policies created incentives for staff to examine student achievement data, to specify linkages between state standards and curriculum, and to follow careful pacing plans to teach these standards in preparation for state tests. As such, this broader policy context shaped the unfolding of reform in the three study districts.

We have not yet discussed the key variable of how the districts' partnership with the IFL contributed to reform. The following chapter examines this topic in more detail, identifying the influence of the IFL on district reform in the four focus areas, as well as its overall influence on the organization and individuals within each district.

CHAPTER SIX

Impact of the Institute for Learning

In this chapter, we look across instructional reform strategies to assess the overall impact of the IFL across the three sites. First, we summarize the relative influence of the IFL on the design and implementation of district strategies in the four areas of reform, and find a relatively stronger reported influence in the area of instructional leadership. Second, we analyze the most influential IFL resources—the Learning Walk and the Principles of Learning—and how they affected the districts. Next, we examine the overall impact of the IFL, and find contributions to the organizational culture and administrative capacity in all three districts. We conclude by presenting a set of common factors that appeared to both constrain and enable partnership efforts and impact. In the end, what emerges in this chapter is less a story about district variation than a set of fairly similar findings across the three districts.

IFL Contribution to the Four Main Areas of Instructional Reform

According to district leaders, the IFL's strongest role was in supporting district efforts to build the instructional leadership of principals and other administrators. In all three districts, leaders felt that the IFL had significantly influenced their decision to focus on instructional leadership, their conception and design of instructional leadership strategies, and the implementation of those efforts. As displayed in Figure 6.1, the reported influence of the IFL was weaker and less consistent across the three districts in the other three areas of reform. The following sections present our findings in more detail.

IFL Made Greatest Contribution to District Instructional Leadership Strategies

As discussed in Chapter Four, in all three districts, the IFL played a prominent role in supporting district policies and programs designed to build the instructional knowledge and leadership skills of administrators. This finding is not surprising because the IFL viewed instructional leadership as central to the reform it sought, and the IFL had developed significant resources in this area. Instructional leadership was the focus of the IFL resident fellows' work in the districts, as well as the materials developed for principal seminars and trainings.

In all three districts, the IFL was reported to influence districts' decisions to invest time and resources in professional development for

Figure 6.1
Reported Role of the IFL in Influencing District Reform Efforts

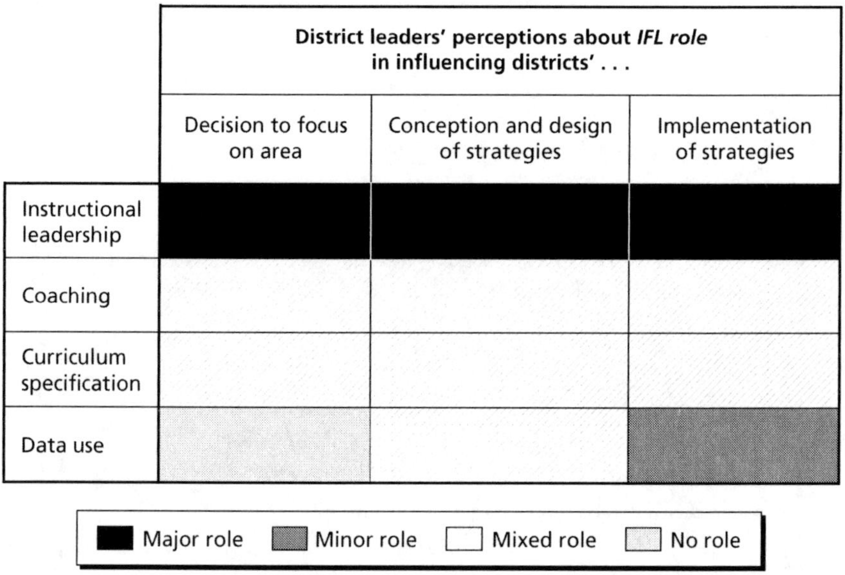

	District leaders' perceptions about *IFL role* in influencing districts' . . .		
	Decision to focus on area	Conception and design of strategies	Implementation of strategies
Instructional leadership	Major role	Major role	Major role
Coaching	Mixed role	Mixed role	No role
Curriculum specification	Mixed role	Mixed role	No role
Data use	No role	No role	Minor role

Major role   Minor role   Mixed role   No role

administrators. For example, the IFL's presentation of research on New York's District 2 was said to influence not only the Monroe superintendent's decision to partner with the IFL but also the district's decision to replicate District 2's strategy of investing in the professional development of principals. Leaders in all three districts said the IFL also helped shape their conceptions of what it meant to be an instructional leader, such as the importance of regularly visiting classrooms and observing instruction. For example, one district leader told us that the main contribution of the IFL was in helping him see that principals were "more than building managers." District leaders also reported that the IFL influenced the actual learning opportunities for administrators. In all three districts, IFL staff regularly helped develop and deliver monthly seminars for principals and provided training opportunities for central office administrators.

Interestingly, in the final year of our study we observed a shift in IFL activity away from instructional leadership to address other district-defined needs. As a result, in all three districts, the IFL was no longer conducting monthly principal seminars as it had done in the past and instead was responding to requests from district leaders for assistance with other areas, such as supporting low-performing schools in Jefferson and the needs of English Language Learners in Monroe. This shift in the IFL's work illustrates how the IFL, as an intermediary organization, attempts to respond to district-defined needs rather than offering a standard, prescribed program of services.

IFL Had Less Influence on Other Areas of Reform

As Figure 6.1 displays, we found that the IFL role in the other areas of instructional improvement was not as strong or consistent across the three districts as its role in the area of instructional leadership. The finding regarding curriculum specification and data use is not surprising because the IFL had developed fewer resources in these areas. However, the relatively weaker reported influence on teacher professional development was surprising because IFL staff viewed their work as focused on promoting professional learning at all levels of the system.

In the area of curriculum specification, the IFL was said to influence only two of the three districts, and this influence was considered quite modest. While IFL staff were reported to have pushed Monroe leaders to see the need to adopt and better specify the district's curriculum and to have helped Roosevelt staff select their math curriculum, they played little reported role in the actual development of curriculum guides (aside from the indirect influence on the insertion of POLs into some of these documents). The use of Learning Walks to monitor curriculum implementation, however, was a key component of both Monroe and Roosevelt's strategies in this area.

In the area of school-based coaching, the IFL played a strong role in designing Roosevelt's literacy coaching program and in training its elementary school literacy coaches. The IFL played a much less significant role in Jefferson's coaching efforts. Jefferson's leaders credit the IFL with demonstrating the value of coaching as an effective model for supporting teacher professional development, but, unlike in Roosevelt, they did not utilize IFL staff or the CFC model to provide the majority of training for their coaches.

Finally, the IFL role was reported to be minimal in the area of data use. None of the three districts attributed their decision to focus on data use strategies to their work with the IFL. Although some Jefferson leaders reported gaining important concepts from the IFL concerning notions of accountability and the importance of benchmarking progress, overall, the IFL was not said to have greatly influenced the design of most data-use strategies. However, the one consistent IFL contribution in this area across all three districts was the Learning Walk, which we discuss in more detail below.

IFL Resources: The Most Influential Ideas and Tools

When partnering with districts, the IFL promises access to a variety of resources to assist with instructional reform—research, materials and tools, networking opportunities, technical assistance, and high-level advice. For the most part, the IFL fulfilled this promise in all three districts. It provided regular off-site meetings; approximately two to three days of resident fellow on-site time per month for planning, training, and support; CD-ROMs, documents, and manuals describing cognitive research on learning and instructional strategies aligned with this research; and time with the IFL director and consultants on an as-needed basis. Although all three districts utilized these various resources, two stood out as particularly prevalent and influential: Learning Walks and the Principles of Learning. District staff across the three districts generally embraced these two resources—unlike other IFL resources—because they addressed local, day-to-day needs and came with specific tools and ongoing professional development that spelled out their purpose and how to use them.

District experiences with two other IFL resources provide a useful contrast to the Learning Walk and POL stories we discuss below. First, although most district leaders reported some value to attending IFL-sponsored meetings—such as gaining uninterrupted time away to reflect on their work and plan for the future, share ideas with individuals from other districts, and learn about core IFL ideas—many administrators complained about the lack of follow-up on those ideas when they returned to the district. As one superintendent noted, "I go off to this thing [the off-site meeting] and when I come back [to the district], I'm [still] doing my thing." Some leaders also wanted more specific guidance on how the work at these off-site meetings was intended to support the individual work with resident fellows on site.

Second, district staff did not embrace the IFL's District Design Principles—a corollary to the Principles of Learning intended to specify the system-level supports needed to scale up standards-based instruction (see Chapter Three for a description)—as widely or enthusiastically as they supported the POLs. In fact, district leaders rarely mentioned these design principles in interviews. The lack of use or perceived usefulness of the design principles is not surprising, given that they are based on a newer, thinner research base (POLs are steeped in a long tradition of cognitive research) and that the IFL did not provide as much specificity and training, or as many supporting materials (e.g., videos, CD ROMs), to help districts understand and put the design principles into practice.

Learning Walks Supported Multiple Instructional Improvement Efforts

Learning Walks were one of the most commonly used IFL tools across the sites. District staff reported greatly appreciating the IFL protocols, rubrics, and training for Learning Walks because they gave concrete information on how to conduct them and what their purpose was. Both within and across districts, however, the purpose, frequency, and perceived impact of the Learning Walks varied greatly.

Purpose. Across the districts, we found administrators using Learning Walks for different purposes to support multiple areas of instructional improvement. In all three districts, Learning Walks were seen as a tool to help district and school leaders identify high-quality instruction and learn how to support teachers or schools needing assistance. All three sites also viewed them as an important source of qualitative data to understand instructional needs. Two of the three districts also used Learning Walks to monitor implementation of district curriculum guides.

Nature and Frequency. Although all three districts conducted various types of Learning Walks, they were reported to be more frequent in Monroe and Roosevelt.[1] External Learning Walks—generally conducted by a group of district leaders or other principals to provide an outside-in view of the quality of instruction across a

---

[1] The IFL expects districts to modify and apply the Learning Walk to local needs and purposes. This variation, however, created some intractable analytic issues for this study. Although our school visits and survey data suggest that Learning Walks occurred more frequently in Monroe and Roosevelt, it is nevertheless difficult to make accurate comparisons across the districts without a clear understanding of how individuals conceptualized the Learning Walk. For example, it is possible that Learning Walks, as defined by the IFL, did not occur more frequently in Roosevelt but rather that individuals in Roosevelt held a looser definition of a Learning Walk. Our qualitative data indicate that Roosevelt may have considered the Learning Walk to be a relatively informal process of walking in and out of classrooms, whereas Monroe and Jefferson may have defined it as a more structured, planned event. These caveats are important to keep in mind when interpreting the survey data on Learning Walks.

school and the status of implementation of district initiatives—were reported to be more common in Monroe and Roosevelt (although they also occurred frequently in the lowest-performing schools in Jefferson). In Monroe, supervisors and principals were often required to conduct a certain number each semester. They were given formal protocols and schedules to follow and were encouraged or required to conduct Learning Walks in schools at different grade-level spans and performance levels. Internal Learning Walks—usually principal-initiated and tied to school needs—were particularly common in Roosevelt, where almost all principals reported conducting them at least once or twice a month. These walks were said to be less formal and not scheduled in advance. In Jefferson, Learning Walks were reported to occur less frequently. As a result of being initially introduced and implemented in a way somewhat contrary to what the IFL intended, these early Learning Walks were seen as evaluating teachers and principals—leading to strong negative reactions from school staff and union officials and the halting of the Learning Walk process for several years early in the partnership.

Perceived Usefulness and Impact. Wide variation in the perceived usefulness and impact of Learning Walks existed within and across the districts. These views often depended on the type and purpose of the Learning Walk. In general, across the three districts, administrators tended to find Learning Walks more useful than teachers did. Teachers often complained that school feedback letters sent to them after Learning Walk were not helpful or relevant to their work. Many teachers also found Learning Walks to be superficial and sometimes overly evaluative. This was particularly true of the more formal and external Learning Walks. Overall, individual "walkers" also tended to find Learning Walks more valuable than did the individuals being observed. In fact, central office administrators in all three districts reported that the walks provided critical information about how district initiatives were working and which schools and principals needed more assistance. Principals and teachers directly participating as walkers reported that on these walks they gleaned new ideas for improving practice. Finally, when Learning Walks were combined with individualized feedback for those teachers observed, the process was reported to be more useful.

Principles of Learning Provided a Common Language

IFL's Principles of Learning—a compilation of cognitive science and research on best practices in standards-based instruction—significantly influenced district reform efforts. In all three districts, we found repeated references to POLs in curriculum guides, district improvement and strategic plans, principals' expectations and evaluation tools (in Monroe and Jefferson), and other materials. Each district also regularly featured POLs in professional development sessions organized for teachers and principals, as well as preparation programs for principals. For example, more than three-quarters of principals responding to surveys in all three districts reported that integrating the POLs into instructional practice was a medium- to high-priority area of professional development offered to teachers at their school.

District and school leaders interviewed in each district repeatedly commented that POLs gave them a framework, as well as a set of shared ideas and vocabulary, for understanding and improving curriculum and instruction. For example, one superintendent described the POLs as the district's "umbrella focus" that helped ensure that teachers were "teaching for quality" instead of "teaching to the test":

> The Principles of Learning to me have been the single thing that set us on course. I think that was the gift and that was grounded in Lauren's research. It is guiding all of our work. It is all over our [curriculum] frameworks. Everything has the Principles of Learning in there.

Similarly, an elementary school principal from another district told us "The Principles of Learning, Clear Expectations, Accountable Talk . . . are overriding strategies and they send a common message . . . a common language about how we begin to discuss curriculum. If we don't share a common language and a common philosophy we are lost." Interview data confirm that POL language was prevalent in all three districts. Throughout the two years of interviews conducted in the three districts, principals and teachers commonly used the terms "accountable talk," "academic rigor," and "clear expectations"—three of the most commonly recognized and emphasized POLs.

Although the POLs influenced the language used in all three districts, individuals at the school level frequently noted that additional support and time were needed to translate these terms into beliefs and practice. As one assistant principal reported, "if the district feels the Principles of Learning are valuable, then there ought to be systematic professional development on those Principles of Learning—instead of sending a disk and saying okay, view this and become familiar with it." We return to the issue of IFL impact on classroom practice later in this chapter.

IFL's Overall Impact on Districts: The Bottom Line

Two overarching findings emerge from our analysis of the IFL impact on district reform. We found that the way the IFL was reported to affect districts was in influencing the broad organizational culture, norms, and beliefs and in helping develop the instructional leadership capacity of administrators. We found less conclusive evidence regarding the IFL's influence on teacher practice.

IFL Had a Strong Reported Impact on Organizational Culture

In all three districts, leaders and administrators reported that the IFL partnership influenced the beliefs and culture of the district overall. One superintendent explained, "I think that the Institute has elevated the level of thinking in the district about how we should be looking at our mission and I think we've used some of the tools and concepts that the Institute has formulated to help us move the agenda to a different level." More specifically, district leaders reported shifts in beliefs and norms around a set of ideas emphasized in IFL materials, professional development, and technical assistance that resonated for them:

- **Effort-based intelligence.** Leaders in all three districts embraced the notion that with effort and proper support, all students could attain high standards. As one superintendent reported, "we believe all kids can be smart if they'll work hard and be supported by a system that sets standards and provides opportunity to learn."
- **Two-way accountability.** The notion of two-way accountability—that all individuals in the system must be accountable to each other and to high standards—was echoed in interviews across the three districts and was especially appreciated by district leaders in each site.
- **Focusing the organization on instruction and learning.** In several districts, we were told that the IFL helped focus the organization and redirect all efforts toward teaching and learning. "Once we were engaged with the IFL, our focus turned toward professional learning for central office, professional learning for principals, professional learning for teachers," said one top administrator.
- **Everyone is a continuous learner.** Leaders frequently noted the importance of considering everyone in the organization a learner. As one administrator explained, "We're trying to model the same thing for principals, that . . . all of us [are] learners. . . . We really buy in to that whole IFL notion of Socializing Intelligence. And that means obviously we as the adults in the district can continue to learn and we have to push each other."
- **Making instruction public.** Many administrators viewed their work with the IFL as changing organizational norms about instruction—most importantly, the idea that instruction was not a private matter, but instead a public endeavor to be observed, discussed, and shared with colleagues. This was particularly true in districts where Learning Walks occurred frequently.

Taken together, these ideas, beliefs, and norms influenced the overall culture of the districts. Some district leaders went so far as to say that they helped districts develop, sustain, and stay focused on a common vision of high-quality teaching and learning. For example, one superintendent referred to the IFL as "the glue that creates a deeper conversation: 'What does [achievement] mean? How do you make that happen in a classroom? What does it look like?'" This leader further noted that while he needed to focus on immediate crises and operational issues, the work with the IFL allowed for a parallel, sustained focus on "deep teaching" that would not have existed otherwise. "I knew that glue would keep us going while I was moving the rest of the system off a dropout list and all the rest"—such as addressing flawed information systems and teacher and principal turnover. He added:

> Don't underestimate the vision thing. It is so important. And I guess [the IFL] helped me because I thought I was pretty clear about my vision but as we began talking Socializing Intelligence, it just helped clearly articulate with theory . . . and CD ROMs. That was very valuable. Because I have those shared beliefs and I believe I've got my organization to at least acknowledge them, but [the IFL's] technology and program really reinforced it.

A study of a business-sponsored intermediary organization similarly found that partnerships altered norms, enhanced coherence of policies, and changed districts' professional culture (Corcoran and Lawrence, 2003).

IFL Was Reported to Affect Administrators' Capacity

IFL partnerships were also reported to influence the knowledge and skills of central office and school administrators. Evidence suggests that the IFL helped build the instructional leadership capacity of administrators across the three districts.

School administrators gained new skills and knowledge from IFL work, but some were concerned about fully utilizing those new ideas, skills, and knowledge. Principals in all three districts generally reported that their work with the IFL had a positive impact. On surveys, we reminded principals that over the past years many professional development opportunities organized by the district had been associated with the IFL—such as Learning Walks and seminars on the POLs—and we asked them how these opportunities had influenced them overall. As Figure 6.2 illustrates, the majority of principals in all three districts felt that these opportunities had improved their skills as instructional leaders and deepened their knowledge about learning. Almost all the principals also reported that the IFL provided them a common language that facilitated dialogue, a finding echoed in a national study of district-intermediary partnerships (Kronley and Handley, 2003).

When interviewed, principals who experienced intensive and direct training with the IFL (e.g., at out-of-district retreats and meetings or in one-on-one mentoring with resident fellows) were more likely to report strong positive impacts on their knowledge, skills, and

Figure 6.2
Principals' Reports on the Impact of IFL-Related Professional Development

Percentage of principals agreeing/strongly agreeing to the statement:
"Overall, IFL-related PD opportunities have . . ."

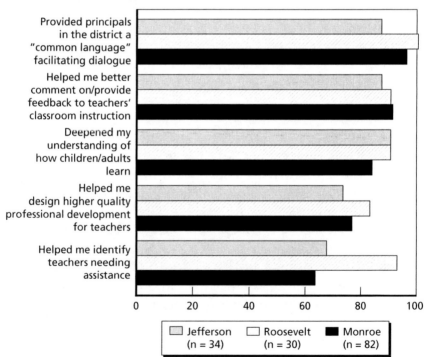

practice. For example, principals reported that their direct work with the IFL had heightened their awareness of what to expect from staff and how to communicate those expectations, how to evaluate teachers, how to recognize good instruction, and what to look for and ask students when observing classrooms. Some attributed changes in their daily practice to the IFL's practical tools and resources. In describing this training, one Roosevelt principal said, "It's been very useful, at least when I go into a classroom I know what to look for . . . it's given me a language to use when I'm giving feedback to teachers about Learning Walks and other issues like that." Similarly, a Jefferson principal explained,

> People who just had that overview coverage and been given the CD on it, they're not there. . . . It wasn't until I started going to Pittsburgh . . . that I really saw how it impacted and made change and talking with my colleagues, not just within [Jefferson] but from throughout the country. . . . I could actually see examples of good teaching. I could see examples of good questioning. I could see examples of high academic rigor. I learned most of those examples when I did those intensive trainings at Pittsburgh.

Despite these generally positive views, some principals expressed frustration with the perceived inability to implement some of the IFL ideas and to push the work deeper into their schools. In one district, principals took issue with the expectation that they should be responsible for training teachers on IFL ideas, noting that they had little time or training to do so. This sentiment was particularly strong among secondary school principals in this particular district.

Central office administrators found value in IFL work but expressed a desire for additional support. District leaders and staff generally reported that IFL staff pushed them to think about and focus on instruction and system-level structures and policies that enabled high-quality instruction. They also felt that the IFL helped them become more knowledgeable about instruction. In addition, many district leaders reported that their work with the IFL improved their skills for supervising and supporting principals—knowing what questions to ask, what to look for when visiting schools, and what assistance to offer after identifying weaknesses. Finally, leaders reiterated that this work gave them a common language that facilitated collaboration and dialogue with colleagues.

Despite these positive reports, many central office administrators struggled with applying IFL ideas. Across the districts, central office staff described IFL work as overly theoretical and requested more concrete support. Some individuals talked about wanting the IFL to "connect the dots," provide more concrete plans, and provide follow-up assistance, particularly for the IFL off-site meetings. One central office administrator reported:

> The only thing I guess I would like more of is . . . how to get things accomplished. I think lots of times the Institute, and that's probably the way it's designed . . . gives the questions, facilitates discussion, but doesn't really give you the answers. Sometimes you'd just like to have more answers or more best practices from this other district, more real examples of how to make things happen, rather than just discussions.

Other district leaders found it difficult to sustain the IFL work when faced with other demands, such as union pressures and accountability requirements. This was particularly true for the two districts with high proportions of low-performing schools.

Finally, the IFL's impact on central office administrators was weakened in all three districts by turnover. When new administrators were hired from outside of the district, they were typically unfamiliar with the IFL's work and were often so busy learning their new responsibilities that it was difficult for IFL staff to gain their attention and buy-in.

Less Evidence to Suggest IFL's Impact on Teachers

As reported throughout this chapter, one of the main IFL impacts we observed across the districts was the adoption of a common language—whether it was teachers and principals citing the POLs to describe high-quality instruction or district leaders espousing broader notions about effort-based intelligence. Although this evidence demonstrates, as one IFL staff member called it, an "intellectual impact," we do not have definitive data to determine whether the IFL had an "action impact" on teacher practice in the three districts.

Teachers interviewed in all three districts were consistently aware of IFL ideas and practices and reported using the POLs in their classrooms—although some frequently noted that these ideas were not new and were simply best practices they had always utilized. And although we heard reports from some teachers of changed practice as a result of their IFL training (e.g., greater use of dialogue with students, greater clarity in defining expectations for students), these reports were inconsistent within and across schools in all three districts. Furthermore, we do not have observational data to confirm or disconfirm these reports.

The majority of teachers responding to surveys across sites reported feeling moderately to very well prepared to utilize POLs in their classroom practice—although more so in Monroe than in the other two districts (81 percent, compared with 66 percent in Roosevelt and 55 percent in Jefferson). This is not surprising given Monroe's more intense focus on turnkeying the IFL ideas to teachers. Yet in many of our interviews across the districts, it was not clear whether all the teachers had the depth of knowledge of IFL concepts that was intended. Their explanations of IFL ideas often revealed confusion, superficial understanding, and possible misinterpretation.

In addition, district and IFL staff readily admitted that they found it challenging to reach teachers and to affect their practice. As one coach explained, the "trickle-down" method of training school leaders to carry the work back to school staff was simply not getting the ideas and knowledge to teachers. In fact, in recent years, IFL leaders have begun experimenting even more with strategies targeted directly at teachers, as opposed to working solely with district and school administrators. For example, in Monroe, the IFL resident fellow met regularly with small groups of teachers to discuss, model, and practice instructional strategies for English Language Learners. This contrasted with the turnkey approach utilized for years in Monroe to train administrators who then trained their staff.

Of course, it is important to keep in mind that we relied primarily on individual reports of influence on practice rather than on direct observations. Further, it is possible that teachers were unaware of the IFL's direct role in district activities and attributed to the district office various activities and outcomes that in fact may have resulted from district staff interactions with the IFL. Also, one might not expect to see or hear about changes in teacher practice in districts where IFL staff were not working directly with teachers, which was certainly the case in some of the study districts throughout the study. Or, at a minimum, we might expect a longer amount of time for IFL ideas to filter down through the various individuals who were directly involved with the IFL, before influencing teacher practice. Even with these alternative explanations and caveats, we nonetheless were left with the impression from limited teacher, administrator, and IFL staff reports that penetration of the POLs and other IFL ideas and practices was inconsistent within each district and not to the deep level desired by the IFL or the districts.

Factors Affecting the IFL's Reported Impact on Districts

Our analysis suggests that several factors are important for understanding the IFL's overall reported impact across districts, as well as its differential effect within particular districts and areas of reform. These factors include

- the capacity of the IFL
- the degree to which leaders at all levels owned and supported the work
- the tendency of districts to view the IFL as a vendor
- trust in the IFL and its perceived credibility
- the use of practical tools
- turnover in district and IFL staff.

These factors collectively explain not only overall impact, but also why the partnerships strengthened and waned over the years.

The IFL Had Limited Capacity—and Possibly Limited Intentions—to Assist Districts with the Full Range of Instructional Improvement Efforts

First and foremost, the IFL had limited resources—staff, skills, experience, and materials—to provide both breadth and depth of support to districts. As a result, the IFL often faced tension between being a generalist that could comprehensively help districts with systemic change on all fronts and a specialist that could provide expert and thorough support in particular areas of emphasis.

When the IFL initially partnered with the three districts, its intent was to assist district and school leaders in transferring knowledge about rigorous standards-based teaching into practice, including how to recognize and support quality teaching and hold teachers accountable for improving their instruction. Over the course of its early work, however, the IFL also recognized the need for districts to develop norms, policies, and structures—characterized in its District Design Principles—to support instructional improvement. However, the IFL's background and expertise remained in the area of teaching and learning and instructional leadership. It is not clear to what degree IFL leaders ever intended to deliver standardized support to districts concerning organizational structures and principles (e.g., how to use data, how to regularly engage with parents and community). As of the end of this study, the IFL had yet to develop a full set of tools or strategies that systematically helped districts with implementing all the design principles.

As discussed earlier in this chapter, the IFL's role in the three districts capitalized on its strengths in the areas of instructional leadership. IFL staff—many of whom were former principals—had extensive knowledge and experience regarding professional development of principals and had produced and honed training materials that assisted districts in the delivery of monthly seminars and other training sessions. But *limited capacity in the other areas of instructional reform greatly constrained the IFL's impact.* In the area of coaching, the IFL had a well-articulated training program for literacy coaches but not for math coaches. While staff attempted to support districts in the areas of curricular specification and data use, IFL's experience and resources in this area were idiosyncratic and much less extensive. As a result, support depended on the knowledge and skills of the individual fellow assigned to a district. In all, the IFL did not have the organizational capacity to support districts in the areas of curriculum guidance and data use as it did for instructional leadership and literacy coaches.

The IFL also had limited capacity to work at all levels of the system, including district leaders, principals, and teachers. IFL leaders and staff acknowledged this limitation up front, noting that approximately two to three fellow-days on site each month was not nearly sufficient for training everyone in a district. Drawing on knowledge of reform efforts that failed because school and district leadership support was lacking, the IFL made a calculated decision to work directly with district leaders, principals, and some teacher leaders. At the same time, it realized that instructional improvement required focused professional development for teachers and therefore decided to pursue a "turnkey" strategy in which IFL staff trained principals who were expected to replicate the training for teachers in their respective schools (in the case of larger districts, such as Monroe, the strategy included an added layer of first training principal supervisors who then "turnkeyed" training to their principals). This strategy met with varying degrees of success, and was deemphasized over time in all three districts.

Nevertheless, the effort to reach teachers remains an ongoing challenge for the IFL. In recent years, IFL staff have experimented with adding new "bottom-up" approaches to scale. In other words, they are working more directly with teachers, who are given leadership opportunities and expected to help spread IFL ideas and practices to colleagues—a strategy recognized as critical to the reform efforts of another intermediary organization (Corcoran and Lawrence, 2003).

Leadership Buy-In at All Levels Enabled Partnership Efforts and Impact

Similar to findings from other research on intermediary organizations (Kronley and Handley, 2003), IFL impact across sites was greatest when top district leaders, such as the superintendent and the deputy superintendent, championed the IFL work and widely communicated their commitment to the partnership. Without direct involvement from top-level leaders, it was often difficult for the IFL to influence the district agenda or to leverage system change. This appeared to be the case in the first years of the partnership in Jefferson, when the superintendent made only a tentative commitment to working with the IFL. As a result, there was reportedly little early buy-in for IFL ideas and activities at lower levels of the system in Jefferson.

On the other hand, when top-level leaders bought into the work, they were able to articulate how the IFL activities aligned with and helped advance other important initiatives. For example, Roosevelt's superintendent wrote a strategic plan that clearly articulated how the district's reform efforts, including the IFL work, coalesced around a common vision. However, when a new Chief Academic Officer was appointed in Roosevelt, he chose not to engage in IFL meetings and activities, implying to others in the district that IFL work was not a priority and was not essential to the district's overall goals. As a result, individuals at all levels of the system reported that the IFL work was marginalized in the year of the partnership that the Chief Academic Officer was there. Similarly, in the later years of the IFL partnerships in Jefferson and Monroe, when district leaders began taking more ownership of the work and directing IFL activities to address local needs concerning low-performing schools and English Language Learners, support and buy-in escalated at all levels of the system. Finally, leadership at lower levels of the system was equally important to the IFL-district partnerships. In our case study visits, we found that supervisors and principals who understood and embraced IFL ideas and activities were much more likely to make them a priority in their practice with those they managed.

The Perception of IFL as a Vendor Hindered Its Effect on District Reform

Without clear support and involvement from top leaders and mid-level staff, the IFL work was more likely to be seen as peripheral, like any other service rendered by a vendor. Despite a shared commitment to being partners and codevelopers with districts, IFL staff in all three districts recognized that central office administrators did not always view them in this way. Across the districts and over time, IFL staff struggled to be understood as more than a vendor. As a partner, the IFL wanted district staff to better understand that they had to take ownership of the work and to share responsibility for the outcomes. According to one IFL staff member: "if they think of us as a vendor, which no matter what we say in the first year, that's what they think of us as, then this accountability on their side just doesn't make sense to them."

Several factors may have contributed to this tension and the widely held perception of the IFL as a vendor. First, districts are generally accustomed to working with outside agencies as vendors. Given districts' pervasive use of outside organizations to provide programs, services, and products needed for school operations and improvement efforts, it is understandable that an organization charging a fee could be viewed in this category of vendorship. Second, the IFL often took on multiple roles within the districts, one of which was a provider of professional development (e.g., districts could purchase specialized training, such as Content-Focused Coaching[SM] or Disciplinary Literacy). If staff within a central office or school came into contact with the IFL in connection with these more specific training activities, they may have conceived of the IFL more narrowly as a vendor.

Finally, while the core package of services entailed a wide range of activities—including not only training but also the provision of tools and materials, policy advice and consultation, and networking opportunities—the majority of *visible* activity was in training and professional development. In other words, when resident fellows did have access to superintendents and participated in planning and consultation, teachers, principals, and even many central office administrators may not have been aware that these interactions were taking place. What they saw and knew about the IFL was a resident fellow leading a seminar on a specific topic—much like any other vendor in a district.

Trust in IFL Staff, Ideas, and Tools, and Their Perceived Credibility, Was Important for Building Teacher, Principal, and District Leader Support

As several authors have noted, the credibility and reputation of an intermediary organization is its "main currency" (Rothman, 2003, p. 6; see also Corcoran and Lawrence, 2003), assuring districts that their investments will pay off and intermediaries that they can sustain and expand their relationships with districts over time. Our research confirms the importance of this perceived legitimacy. To the extent that teachers and principals viewed the IFL, its ideas, and tools as an effective means for achieving their goals, they were more likely to embrace the IFL work.

First, it was important for school staff to view individuals working for the IFL as knowledgeable and experienced with administration and teaching in their local context (e.g., in their type of community, school, subject area, and student population). IFL staff had more credibility when they had experience at all levels of the system, including the classroom, school administration, and district administration. Furthermore, when a resident fellow's area of expertise matched the district's need—such as the Monroe fellow's experience as a top-level administrator and expertise around language acquisition—there was greater opportunity for synergy and influence. However, when school staff questioned the relevance of IFL tools to their student population or the qualifications of individual IFL staff to guide work in these settings, support for IFL ideas and activities waned.

Related to credibility was the level of trust that existed between IFL and district and school staff. Both district and IFL respondents suggested that this type of partnership required time spent on building relationships and that trust built over time greatly facilitated the work. In each district the resident fellows invested heavily in relationship-building efforts, and to varying degrees found these efforts to be valuable in gaining access to district meetings and opportunities to work side by side with administrators to shape district policies. In contrast, perceptions that the IFL threatened existing routines greatly limited its work. In interviews, IFL staff repeatedly recognized that their struggle to be embraced as partners may have been hampered by IFL's potential or perceived threat to district administrators' professional expertise and power. "It's really threatening to have us come and make the types of decisions that [central office administrators] have had autonomy over previously," admitted one resident fellow.

Practical Tools Supported Application of IFL Ideas but Raised Concerns About Superficial Implementation

As we reported earlier in this chapter, Learning Walks were widely used because they were a practical tool for examining instruction. Learning Walks included a formal protocol for achieving the theoretical goal of "getting into classrooms" by providing guidance to school and district leaders on every step, including how to inform teachers of a pending classroom visit, what to look for while observing the classroom, how to discuss observations in a positive and productive manner, and how to provide feedback to teachers. Similarly, the IFL provided a number of tools to support use of the Principles of Learning, including CD-ROMs, handouts, and training materials for administrators to use with teachers. Respondents at all levels reported that the practicality of these tools and resources facilitated their use and promoted deeper understanding of underlying IFL theories and ideas. A study of district-intermediary partnerships similarly found that practical tools developed by the intermediary, such as rubrics and assessments, were critical for reinforcing desired norms (Corcoran and Lawrence, 2003).

Nevertheless, some individuals in all three districts desired even more-practical materials and support, and often complained about the overly theoretical nature of IFL work. As one district leader put it,

> What I'd like to do is come away with a set of tools each time. Here's a tool you give a principal to work on writing to get more accountable talk. See this is what we're not getting. It's still very generic. There's not the scaffolding, I'm not talking mindless prescription but I'm talking some scaffolding. Give me the question set that I should use and give me some examples of what good conversations look like.

Yet the desire for more concrete tools and strategies presented a dilemma for IFL and district staff. In several districts, there was some concern that this desire for tools and the tendency to grab onto physical manifestations of how to demonstrate IFL ideas in a school or classroom led to more-superficial applications as opposed to a deep understanding or application of these ideas. For example, many teachers and administrators noted that simply placing a criteria chart or rubric on a bulletin board did not necessarily translate into instructional practice aligned with the Principles of Learning. Moreover, some feared that district practices to monitor the presence of these physical manifestations or to create more specified, concrete expectations served to "proceduralize" and undermine the value of the IFL partnership and its ideas. The dilemma of wanting concrete tools and practical ideas to help implement and spread IFL ideas, yet fearing the inauthentic translation of IFL ideas and theory, lingered in the three districts. This tension is not new, and its existence in theory-based change efforts is well recognized (McLaughlin and Mitra, 2001).

In fact, IFL staff themselves recognized the propensity for new users to dilute the intended rationale, ideas, and meaning embedded in various tools. For this reason, the coupling of ongoing professional development, technical assistance, and other supporting materials with IFL tools—such as study groups led by a resident fellow in which participants practiced using the tool, and videotapes and CD ROMs demonstrating teachers and administrators using the tools—became an important means for ensuring more-authentic implementation of IFL tools, such as the Learning Walk and Principles of Learning.

Turnover Challenged IFL Efforts to Sustain and Deepen Reform

Like most urban school systems, the three study districts faced high levels of turnover among teachers, principals, and even central office administrators. As a result, many new staff members were less familiar with IFL ideas—this was particularly true for new teachers across all three districts and some principals and top-level central office staff. This turnover clearly affected the ability to sustain IFL work, which by design requires intensive training and opportunities for conversation, deep study, and practice over time. In all three districts and at all levels, we heard concerns about how to include new staff and bring them up to speed while not repeating the same training for veterans. Similarly, turnover among IFL resident fellows may have disrupted partnership momentum over time. For example, new fellows arriving in a district often had to start anew to build relationships and trust.

Summary

This chapter has described the impact of the IFL on district instructional improvement efforts and the factors that appeared to affect these outcomes. In all three districts, the IFL made its strongest reported contribution in the area of systemwide efforts to build the instructional leadership of administrators—influencing not only the design and implementation of professional development opportunities for principals and central office staff but also the reported knowledge, skills, and beliefs of those administrators. According to district leaders and staff, the IFL also affected the organizational culture and norms within the three districts. The evidence of IFL impact on teachers, however, was limited by the design and focus of this study and merits further research.

Over time, several factors emerged that explain the ebb and flow of each partnership. The IFL's reported impact was particularly strong when

- top-level leaders championed the IFL work and visibly supported it
- district staff were actively engaged in co-constructing and customizing the IFL work to meet local needs
- IFL staff were viewed as trustworthy and credible, possessing expertise that matched a particular district need
- the IFL offered practical tools and resources to support implementation of theoretical ideas.

In contrast, the IFL's influence was marginalized when the IFL was treated as a vendor—providing particular services without much coordination and support from district leaders. Even in the best of times, the partnerships were constrained by the IFL's limited capacity to support districts in all their instructional improvement efforts and by the enduring problem of turnover within the district and the IFL.

CHAPTER SEVEN

Conclusions and Lessons Learned

The purpose of this study was to analyze the instructional improvement efforts of three urban districts engaged in partnerships with the Institute for Learning (IFL). The study sought to answer four broad questions:

1. What strategies did districts employ to promote instructional improvement? How did these strategies work?
2. What were the constraints and enablers of district instructional improvement efforts?
3. What was the impact of the IFL? What were the constraints and enablers of the district-IFL partnerships?
4. What are the implications for district instructional improvement and district-intermediary partnerships?

The following sections summarize the main findings of the study and our answers to these questions. Although the first three questions have been addressed in previous chapters and will be summarized below, we reflect on the final question for the first time at the end of this chapter.

Summary of Findings

In answer to question 1, we found that district approaches to instructional reform converged on four common areas of focus:

- building the instructional leadership of principals;
- supporting the professional learning of teachers, primarily through on-site coaching in two districts
- providing greater specification for standards-aligned curriculum
- promoting the use of data to guide instructional decisions.

Although all three districts pursued activities within all these areas, each district tended to focus on two key areas to leverage change throughout the system. In addition, the districts achieved varying degrees of success in attaining the intermediate goals for these reform initiatives.

In answer to the second research question, we found that a number of common factors constrained and enabled instructional improvement efforts across districts. Although it was important for districts to implement a set of reforms that treated instruction comprehensively, districts benefited from focusing on a small number of initiatives. District success was also tied to the degree to which strategies

- were aligned with other existing or new programs
- enabled multiple stakeholders to engage in reform
- found an appropriate balance between standardization and flexibility
- were enforced by local accountability incentives for meaningful change to instructional practice.

Finally, insufficient capacity—related to time, fiscal resources, and district staff—hindered instructional improvement efforts; assistance from knowledgeable district staff and on-site instructional specialists, when available, enabled district work.

The third research question asked what impact the IFL had on instructional reform efforts. Relative to the other areas of reform, the IFL made its strongest contributions in the area of systemwide efforts to build the instructional leadership of administrators in all three districts—specifically, by influencing the design and implementation of professional development opportunities for principals and central office staff.

Overall, in all three districts, the IFL was reported to affect the organizational culture, norms, and beliefs about instruction. According to district staff, the IFL also helped develop the knowledge and skills of administrators. Both of these reported impacts addressed key challenges facing districts undertaking systemic reform: a lack of alignment among district initiatives and limited capacity to undertake reform. By providing a common language and set of ideas, the IFL may have helped districts build mutually supportive reform strategies based on a common vision of high-quality instruction. By enhancing principals' and central office administrators' knowledge and skills, the IFL also helped build the overall capacity of the district to lead instructional change across the system of schools.

We also found that several common factors influenced IFL partnerships with and impact on the districts:

- leadership buy-in, trust in, and perceived credibility of the IFL
- alignment between IFL expertise and district needs
- availability of practical tools
- the degree to which the IFL was viewed as a vendor
- IFL capacity
- staff turnover.

Lessons Learned for Policy and Practice

As more and more policymakers, researchers, and reformers recognize the important role of school districts, particularly in the era of high-stakes accountability, the notion of district capacity and capacity-building has become—and will continue to be—an important policy problem. As increasing numbers of schools and districts are labeled "low performing" or "in need of improvement" and districts and schools face state sanctions, districts are likely to examine and experiment with strategies similar to those described in this study. State departments of education—required under NCLB to assist districts "in need of improvement"—also are probably seeking information on how to effect districtwide change. Many districts, particularly those with limited internal capacity, may seek outside assistance for improving teaching and learning. As such, intermediary organizations like the Institute for Learning could play a central role in addressing the needs of districts.

As noted previously, readers should keep in mind the limitations of our study, including the limited sample of three districts, the low teacher response rates, the lack of direct measures of teaching and learning, and the lack of longitudinal survey data. Even though our data have some limitations and we lack definitive evidence to suggest that the lessons learned in these three districts can be generalized to other districts or intermediary partnerships, the experiences nonetheless may provide important insights for policymakers and practitioners seeking districtwide improvement, as well as organizations seeking to enter the intermediary "market." Accordingly, we offer two sets of lessons: one for instructional improvement and one for district-intermediary partnerships.

Lessons for Instructional Improvement

Based on the reform experiences of the three study districts, we offer the following lessons learned to districts, states, private funders, and other policymakers.

Investing in the professional development of central office staff can enhance their capacity to lead instructional reform. In all three districts, the capacity, knowledge, and skills of central office administrators (e.g., curriculum specialists, individuals supervising principals) greatly influenced districts' abilities to develop and implement coherent instructional improvement strategies and to spread and support work at the school level. Recent research similarly affirms the important role of mid-level staff and recommends that district leaders "invest in ongoing professional development for mid-level managers so that staff learn to more effectively support schools, to deepen their knowledge about teaching and learning, and to integrate their work with other central office departments" (Burch and Spillane, 2004, p. 6). Thus, districts might consider providing regular professional development opportunities for central office staff. As we found with the IFL, intermediary organizations could assist districts in providing or shaping those professional development efforts. States could also play a role, expanding professional development opportunities through regional support structures or on-site technical assistance (both of which generally focus on the learning needs of teachers and principals).

Instituting local accountability policies that create incentives for meaningful change can promote implementation. As districts add additional accountability systems and requirements to monitor the progress of their schools, they might consider taking into account the nature of the incentives created. For example, although some of the study districts used Learning Walks to monitor the use of curriculum guides and hold teachers accountable for high-quality instruction, these walks often created incentives for teachers to show superficial implementation of the reforms rather than deep integration of the concepts into their teaching. Yet, when Learning Walks were coupled with pre- and post-walk conferences in which groups of teachers and administrators discussed what was observed and collectively reflected on feedback, the experience was seen as useful not only for the administrators monitoring practice but also for the teachers who saw Learning Walks as a means to improve their practice.

Aligning and developing a comprehensive set of strategies can reinforce overarching instructional improvement goals. As we learned in all three districts, district actions can sometimes be perceived by school staff to conflict with one another, particularly with regard to demands on time and resources. For example, principals in Jefferson reported receiving conflicting messages from district leaders regarding their roles and responsibilities. They were often unsure of how to prioritize their time. When districts designed instructional improvement efforts to reinforce one another and leaders communicated this intended alignment, school staff were more inclined to see how multiple demands on their time could collectively further the goal of improving student achievement. For example, rather than viewing analysis of student data and classroom observation as two distinct responsibilities, principals in Monroe explained to us how both practices were important for monitoring and supporting instructional improvement.

Comprehensiveness was also important to successful rollout and implementation of district efforts. Rather than implementing curriculum guides as a stand-alone initiative, all three districts benefited from pursuing multiple actions to support the broader area of curriculum specification by offering teachers professional development related to curriculum guides, tasking coaches and school leaders with supporting the use of the guides, and providing supporting materials and assessments.

Our findings suggest additional lessons for the four areas of reform. With regard to the four areas of instructional improvement analyzed in this study, we offer the following lessons:

Instructional leadership. Although all three districts invested in professional development opportunities for principals and clearly expected principals to move beyond operational management, they did not remove all the structural barriers to achieving this new leadership vision. Districts might consider investing in strategies that free up principals' time to engage in instructional leadership practices or redefine job descriptions and responsibilities so that other individuals share responsibilities for leading the school (e.g., see Spillane, Halverson, and Diamond, 1999 and 2001, for further discussion of distributed leadership practices). For example, districts could try to reduce off-site meetings and paperwork requirements, or assign assistant principals or office managers to student discipline and administrative tasks so that principals have more time to devote to instructional matters.

Coaching. In each of the study districts, the availability of on-site instructional experts benefited teachers and principals. Districts might consider investing in such a strategy by creating clearly defined, site-specific coaching positions to promote school-level instructional capacity. Such positions could also further other district instructional initiatives.

Curriculum specification. Although guides were reported to yield several benefits (e.g., greater consistency of instruction), taken alone, they were not said to meaningfully influence the "craft" of teaching. Districts might consider involving teachers in the development and revisions of these documents, delivering the guides in a timely manner, and providing ongoing professional development to assist teachers in building the pedagogical skills to support the effective use of guides in classrooms.

Data use. One challenge facing all three districts was the need for timely data presented in a user-friendly format that could readily benefit teachers in their daily instruction. To address this challenge, administrators might consider offering more support to help teachers analyze and interpret data and identify strategies to address diagnosed problems. Such support could include giving teachers focused training, and tasking individuals to work with teachers to "filter" data or make them easier to interpret. Districts might also consider investing in assessments that yield more frequent and timely data that teachers perceive to be valid, useful, and not time-consuming.

Lessons for District-Intermediary Partnerships

As noted in Chapter Two, the IFL represents a specific class of intermediary organization: It is *imported* (not located in the community), it charges a fee for its services, and it arrives in districts with a specific theory of action and set of ideas and tools. And although these specific characteristics set it apart from other types of third-party organizations, the experiences of the IFL in these three districts nevertheless provide potentially useful insights for other intermediary organizations as well as for districts considering partnerships with similar organizations. We offer the following observations.

Buy-in and support from top-level leaders can affect partnership viability. The IFL partnerships we studied thrived in districts where superintendents took ownership of the work and signaled support of the work to everyone in the system. Intermediary organizations also might consider building relationships over time not only with superintendents but also with other top- and mid-level administrators to develop trust and a shared sense of responsibility. This may be particularly true for intermediary organizations that are likely to be perceived by central office and school staff as not understanding district needs or having district interests in mind (e.g., an elite university, a for-profit company).

Preexisting reform initiatives and partnerships are important to consider when forming partnerships. When defining goals and designing activities, it is worth taking into account the breadth and array of reform efforts and partners already existing in the district. Like the three cases studied, districts often partner with multiple external organizations and experiment with a variety of reforms—new curricular or professional development programs, reorganizations, or arrangements for consultants to assist with various activities. Given these possible competing interests and ideas, an intermediary organization could work at coordinating the various activities in ways that promote a consistent vision of high-quality instruction and provide clear direction to school staff.

The capacity of the intermediary organization and its alignment with district needs can greatly affect partnership success. Organizations seeking to partner with districts might consider their own capacity to support districts (e.g., who they hire; their experience, background, and skills; and how much time they are able to spend on site) and the extent to which this capacity matches district needs. As we found in the three study districts, without a match between capacity and needs, intermediary organizations risk being relegated to vendor status and seen as tangential to the district's core reform efforts. The more that intermediary staff and activities were perceived to meet district needs and further district goals, the more attention, buy-in, and support they received. Intermediaries might also think about tradeoffs between breadth (helping districts with all areas of need and working to have an effect on all schools at once) and depth (focusing on areas where they have greatest expertise and starting on a smaller scale and expanding work over time).

Practical tools are needed that are considered relevant and legitimate to the district's local context. Intermediary organizations might consider the extent to which the materials and tools they bring into districts reflect and apply to the student and teacher population, as well as other contextual factors of the partner district. They might also consider the extent to which intermediary staff provide sufficient scaffolding—training, follow-up, mentoring, and concrete tools—to enable administrators and teachers to translate intermediary ideas and theory into deep meaning and practice.

Multiple types of "scale-up" strategies can be relevant to systemwide change efforts. As we have discussed, the IFL initially started with the top-down approach of working with central office administrators and principals, expecting the work to trickle down to the classroom level. Over time, the IFL increasingly recognized the value of adding the bottom-up approach of working more directly with teachers.[1] Thus, new organizations seeking to partner with districts might consider both approaches: Teachers would then have direct exposure to the ideas and strategies, but district leaders would understand them well enough to create supportive structures and policies that enable teachers to use those ideas and strategies in their daily practice.

Defining and measuring partnership goals and progress may facilitate improvements and sustained partnerships over time. Districts and intermediaries might consider identifying interim and long-term measures of success at the outset of the partnership. In a summative sense, this information can help both parties ensure ongoing stakeholder support and funding. In a formative sense, the data can help the partnership gauge progress and learn to improve its efforts (a recommendation echoed by Kronley and Handley, 2003). In many ways, RAND's research has been used in the three districts and in the IFL for both of these purposes. In interviews, IFL and district staff did not use this exact language about evaluating the partnerships' success; thus, we have not discussed it earlier in this report. Nonetheless, we offer the following observation as a possible means to address sev-

---

[1] Another intermediary organization, the Bay Area School Reform Collaborative or BASRC (recently renamed Springboard Schools), which aimed to affect districtwide instructional improvement, experienced the opposite evolution over time: It worked directly and almost exclusively at the school level in the early years and then, over time, realized the importance of also working at the district level (McLaughlin and Talbert, 2004). As one BASRC leader explained, "While BASRC began with a focus on building organizational capacity in schools, the goal of sustainability led to the need to build organizational capacity in school district central offices as well" (Vargo, 2004, p. 595). As such, the organization now provides coaching and support at both the district and school levels.

eral issues that emerged throughout the course of this study. Measuring interim and long-term success could help districts and intermediaries better define their goals and responsibilities, as well as keep all partners focused on progress being made. These data might also help intermediaries to be seen as partners rather than vendors and to articulate more clearly the systemic role they seek to play and the degree to which they are having an impact. Evaluating progress and outcomes could also assist intermediaries and districts with important resource decisions, such as identifying staff to match district needs or considering when to end partnerships. This task is not easy. It is challenging to measure the success of an intermediary organization and to isolate its effect in districts that are also engaged in numerous other reform efforts, often with multiple partners. Measuring effect is further complicated by the fact that the IFL's strategy—and possibly the strategy of many other intermediaries—of co-constructing reform efforts with district leaders leads to variation in the activities and general rollout of IFL work, so that there is no standard intervention or model across different contexts.

Conclusion

The experiences of these three urban districts and their partnerships with the IFL are evidence of promising results from systemwide instructional improvement efforts, but they also serve to caution districts and intermediary organizations about the challenges they may face when attempting similar reforms. Of course, our results are not definitive and cannot be generalized to other districts or intermediaries. Yet the data gathered in these three case studies suggest that urban districts can, in fact, facilitate changes at scale—particularly greater uniformity of curriculum and use of data to inform instructional decisions. Our case studies also show that it is possible for an intermediary organization to assist districts in addressing a persistent constraint to reform by building the capacity of district staff to engage in instructional change. Central office and school administrators consistently reported that the IFL gave them a common language, as well as knowledge and skills to help them lead instructional change.

However, our research also illustrates that many obstacles and unanswered questions remain to achieving widescale improvements in teaching and learning in urban districts. Insufficient capacity—most notably time, staff, and funding—was reported to greatly constrain the reform efforts in the three sites. In addition, perceived misalignment of policies and lack of flexibility, along with accountability incentives that reward superficial implementation, challenged efforts to enact change across a school system. The study also raises many questions for future research. For example, once the IFL, or any intermediary, formally ends a partnership, how and to what extent do districts sustain the work? How do particular improvement strategies affect teacher practice and student achievement? What are the long-term effects of district decisions to invest resources in one area of reform over another? Answers to these questions, and more, can further expand our understanding of how to improve urban school systems, erase persistent student achievement gaps, and achieve federal proficiency goals.

Survey Instruments

On the following pages we reproduce the surveys we designed to be administered to teachers and principals in each district.

District Instructional Improvement Efforts:
TEACHER SURVEY

RAND, an independent research organization with funding from the Hewlett Foundation, is conducting a study of instructional reform efforts of three urban school districts. The purpose of this survey is to obtain teachers' views on instructional improvement efforts taking place within your school and district, and to assist your district and others in making improvements to these efforts. It's important that all individuals in your school participate in this survey so that results will fairly represent the opinions and experiences of teachers in your school. Completing this survey is voluntary, but the information you provide will be critical for understanding the nature and impact of district reform efforts.

RAND will keep your responses strictly confidential. Once sealed into the reply envelope, no one at your school or district will see the completed survey. Results of the survey will be reported only in summary statistical form so that neither individuals nor their schools can be identified. We will not disclose your identity or information that identifies you to anyone outside the research project.

The survey should take approximately 20 minutes to complete. Please use a No. 2 pencil to fill out the survey. If you have any questions or concerns regarding this survey you can contact the person below for clarification. After you are finished, please mail your survey back in the envelope provided.

THANK YOU, in advance, for your time and input.

PLEASE DO NOT WRITE IN THIS AREA

- Use a No. 2 pencil only.
- Do not use ink, ballpoint, or felt tip pens.
- Make solid marks that fill the circle completely.
- Erase cleanly any marks you wish to change.
- Make no stray marks on this form.
- Do not fold, tear, or mutilate this form.

CORRECT MARK ●   **INCORRECT MARKS** ⊘⊗◔⊙

1. Are you a classroom teacher? (Mark one.)

A "classroom teacher" includes teachers with direct responsibilities for teaching students, for example, teachers of academic and/or elective courses, special education teachers, resource teachers, and ESL teachers. This does not include teacher aides, student teachers, long- or short-term substitutes, paraprofessionals, full-time coaches, and other non-teaching professionals such as nurses or guidance counselors.

○ 1 Yes, I am a full-time classroom teacher.
○ 2 Yes, I am a part-time classroom teacher (i.e. I do not have a full teaching load). ➡ *When completing the survey, please refer to your experiences as a classroom teacher.*
○ 3 No, I am not a classroom teacher. ➡ *You do not need to continue filling out this survey. Please enclose and mail survey in envelope provided. Thank you for your time.*

2. Do you teach at more than one school in this district?
○ No
○ Yes ➡ *When completing this survey, please refer to your experiences at the school where you received this survey.*

3. What grade levels and subject areas do you teach at this school this year? (Mark all that apply.)

a. Grade levels

○ Pre-K   ○ 7
○ K   ○ 8
○ 1   ○ 9
○ 2   ○ 10
○ 3   ○ 11
○ 4   ○ 12
○ 5   ○ Ungraded
○ 6

b. Subjects

○ Multiple subjects, self-contained classroom
OR:
○ English/reading/language arts
○ Mathematics
○ Science
○ Social studies/history
○ Other: _____

4. Do you teach... (Mark one answer per row.)
a. ...a designated special education class? ○ Yes ○ No
b. ...a designated ESL class? ○ Yes ○ No
c. ...a designated honors, Advanced Placement, or Gifted and Talented class? ○ Yes ○ No

5. Please estimate the number of students you teach in a typical week in the following categories. (Fill in each space with zero or another number.)

a. Total number of students

b. Students classified as English as a second language learners (ESL students)

c. Students classified as special education students with Individualized Education Plans (IEPs)

d. Students pulled out of regular class for remedial instruction

CURRICULUM AND INSTRUCTION

6. Is there one or more district curriculum guide(s) relevant to your teaching assignment? (Mark one.)

	One	Two	Three	Four	More than 4
	①	②	③	④	⑤

○ 1 Yes ➡ If so, how many?
○ 2 No ➡ *Go to Question 8*
○ 3 Not sure ➡ *Go to Question 8*

7. Please indicate the extent to which you agree or disagree with the following statements about the curriculum guide(s) relevant to your teaching assignment. (Mark one number in each row.)

	Strongly Disagree	Disagree	Agree	Strongly Agree	Don't Know
a. The curriculum guide(s) promote consistency of instruction <u>among classes</u> at the same grade level.	①	②	③	④	⓪
b. The curriculum guide(s) promote continuity of instruction <u>between grades</u>.	①	②	③	④	⓪
c. The curriculum guide(s) and supporting materials (including textbooks) are aligned with each other.	①	②	③	④	⓪
d. The curriculum guide(s) are too inflexible to effectively teach my students.	①	②	③	④	⓪
e. The curriculum guide(s) include more content than can be covered adequately in the school year.	①	②	③	④	⓪
f. The curriculum guide(s) are too rigorous for most of the students I teach.	①	②	③	④	⓪
g. I regularly use the curriculum guide(s) in planning my lessons.	①	②	③	④	⓪
h. The curriculum guide(s) provide useful suggestions for assessing student progress (e.g., end of unit tests/projects).	①	②	③	④	⓪
i. The curriculum guide(s) provide useful suggestions about instructional strategies (i.e. how to group students, how to individualize instruction).	①	②	③	④	⓪
j. The curriculum guide(s) appropriately address the needs of special student populations (e.g., English as a second language learners (ESL), students with IEPs).	①	②	③	④	⓪
k. It is unclear how the Principles of Learning are intended to support or fit in with the curriculum guide(s).	①	②	③	④	⓪
l. The curriculum guide(s) help me prepare my students for the state tests.	①	②	③	④	⓪
m. There were <u>opportunities</u> for me to provide feedback to the district about the curriculum guide(s) during their development.	①	②	③	④	⓪
n. Feedback from teachers was <u>incorporated</u> into the curriculum guide(s) during their development and revision.	①	②	③	④	⓪

PROFESSIONAL DEVELOPMENT

Questions 8-11 ask about school- and district-sponsored activities to support your professional growth and development.

8. During the current school year (including last summer), how many times did you engage in each of the following types of professional development activities? If you engaged in an activity, overall how valuable was each activity for your own professional development? (Mark one number for frequency and, if you engaged in the activity, one for value in each row.)

	Frequency of activity					Overall value of activity for your professional development (if engaged in an activity)			
	Never	A few times a year	Once or twice a month	Once or twice a week	Daily or almost daily	Not Valuable	Minimally Valuable	Moderately Valuable	Very Valuable
a. School-based professional development activities for teachers at your school (e.g., seminars, training sessions)	①	②	③	④	⑤	①	②	③	④
b. Professional development activities involving teachers across schools in your district (e.g., grade level or content area meetings, districtwide training sessions)	①	②	③	④	⑤	①	②	③	④
c. Observing another teacher for at least 30 minutes at a time	①	②	③	④	⑤	①	②	③	④
d. Receiving feedback from another teacher who observed in your class	①	②	③	④	⑤	①	②	③	④
e. Participating in a Learning Walk at your school or another school in the district	①	②	③	④	⑤	①	②	③	④
f. Participating in a formal coaching or mentoring relationship with another teacher or staff member	①	②	③	④	⑤	①	②	③	④
g. Collaborating with other teachers (e.g., planning lessons, discussing common challenges, analyzing student work)	①	②	③	④	⑤	①	②	③	④

9. Now think about the <u>content</u> of school- and district-sponsored activities to support <u>your</u> professional growth and development.

Considering the amount of time you spent participating in these professional development activities in the current school year (including last summer), how much <u>emphasis</u> was placed on the following areas? If emphasized, how <u>useful</u> was the professional development received in each area for your work as a teacher? (Mark one number for emphasis and, if emphasized, one for usefulness in each line.)

	Amount of emphasis in the training and support you received from the school/district				Usefulness of training and support (if emphasized)			
	No Emphasis	Minor Emphasis	Moderate Emphasis	Major Emphasis	Not Useful	Minimally Useful	Moderately Useful	Very Useful
a. Standards, content, and instruction relevant to your teaching assignment	①	②	③	④	①	②	③	④
b. Instructional strategies for English as a second language (ESL) students	①	②	③	④	①	②	③	④
c. Instructional strategies for special education students (i.e., students with IEPs)	①	②	③	④	①	②	③	④
d. Familiarizing students with state test format and test-taking strategies	①	②	③	④	①	②	③	④
e. Integrating the Principles of Learning into your instructional practice	①	②	③	④	①	②	③	④
f. Implementing district curriculum guide(s)	①	②	③	④	①	②	③	④
g. Reviewing and implementing your school's improvement plan	①	②	③	④	①	②	③	④
h. Interpreting and using reports of student test results	①	②	③	④	①	②	③	④

10. How <u>well prepared</u> do you feel to perform the following tasks? (Mark one number in each row.)

	Not well Prepared	Minimally Prepared	Moderately Prepared	Very well Prepared	N/A
a. Understanding and implementing the curriculum guide(s)	①	②	③	④	⓪
b. Implementing your school improvement plan	①	②	③	④	⓪
c. Interpreting and using reports of student test results	①	②	③	④	⓪
d. Utilizing the Principles of Learning in classroom practice	①	②	③	④	⓪
e. Participating in Learning Walks	①	②	③	④	⓪
f. Preparing your students to perform better on the state assessments	①	②	③	④	⓪

11. Please indicate the extent to which you agree or disagree with the following statements about the school- and district-sponsored professional development activities in which you participated in the current school year (including last summer). (Mark one number in each row.)

Overall, the professional development activities I participated in this year. . .	Strongly Disagree	Disagree	Agree	Strongly Agree	Don't Know
a. Deepened my knowledge of the subject matter I teach	①	②	③	④	⓪
b. Increased my ability to set and communicate clear expectations for student work	①	②	③	④	⓪
c. Were a series of single events with little or no follow-up	①	②	③	④	⓪
d. Improved my skills to meet the instructional needs of all the students I teach (e.g., English as a second language learners, special education students, students from diverse cultural backgrounds)	①	②	③	④	⓪
e. Were developed with teacher input	①	②	③	④	⓪
f. Were generally a waste of my time	①	②	③	④	⓪
g. Improved my ability to involve students in active reasoning and problem-solving	①	②	③	④	⓪
h. Were designed or chosen to support the school's needs or improvement goals	①	②	③	④	⓪
i. Were designed or chosen to support the implementation of district-wide initiatives (e.g., curriculum guide(s), Principles of Learning)	①	②	③	④	⓪

USE OF DATA FOR PLANNING AND INSTRUCTION

12. If the following sources of information were available to you this year, how useful were they for guiding instruction in your classroom(s)? (Mark one number in each row.)

	Not Available	Available and. . .			
		Not Useful	Minimally Useful	Moderately Useful	Very Useful
a. School-wide student performance results on state test(s)	①	②	③	④	⑤
b. Your students' performance results on state test(s) disaggregated by student groups (e.g., grade level, classrooms, student characteristics)	①	②	③	④	⑤
c. Your students' performance results on state test(s) disaggregated by subtopic or skill	①	②	③	④	⑤
d. Your students' performance on district assessments	①	②	③	④	⑤
e. Information gained from Learning Walk(s) (e.g., letter or presentation from the principal)	①	②	③	④	⑤
f. Results of systematic review(s) of student work	①	②	③	④	⑤

13. **Does your school have a school improvement plan for this school year? (Mark one.)**
   ○ 1 Yes
   ○ 2 No ➡ *Go to Question 17*
   ○ 3 Don't Know ➡ *Go to Question 17*

14. **How familiar are you with the contents of this year's school improvement plan? (Mark one.)**
   ○ 1 Not familiar at all
   ○ 2 Heard the plan discussed, but never looked at it
   ○ 3 Skimmed the plan
   ○ 4 Read the plan and have a thorough understanding of it

15. **Were you on the team that developed the school improvement plan for this school year? (Mark one.)**
   ○ 1 Yes
   ○ 2 No

16. **To what extent do you agree or disagree with the following statements about your <u>school improvement plan</u> and the <u>planning process</u>. (Mark one number in each row.)**

	Strongly Disagree	Disagree	Agree	Strongly Agree	Don't Know
a. My input was solicited in the school improvement planning process.	①	②	③	④	⓪
b. The district provides clear and consistent guidance for the development of our school improvement plan.	①	②	③	④	⓪
c. The school improvement plan shapes decisions made at my school.	①	②	③	④	⓪
d. The school improvement plan has influenced my teaching.	①	②	③	④	⓪
e. The school improvement plan is something that we only use to comply with district or state requirements.	①	②	③	④	⓪
f. The district monitors the degree to which our school improvement plan has been implemented.	①	②	③	④	⓪
g. The information we get from the plan is not worth the time it takes to produce it.	①	②	③	④	⓪

17. **Which of the following characterizes your school? (Mark one answer in each row.)**

	Yes	No	Don't Know	
a. My school met <u>all</u> **Adequate Yearly Progress (AYP) requirements** for the 2002-03 school year.	○	○	○	➡ *"Adequate yearly progress" is the amount of yearly improvement each school is expected to make under state accountability provisions.*
b. My school was identified as **"in need of improvement"** by the state in 2002-03.	○	○	○	➡ *Schools that fail to make adequate yearly progress, as defined by their state, for two consecutive years, are identified as "in need of improvement" under federal accountability provisions.*

DISTRICT AND SCHOOL CONTEXT

18. **To what extent is each of the following a challenge to improving teaching and learning in your classroom? (Mark one number in each row.)**

	Not a Challenge	A Minor Challenge	A Moderate Challenge	A Great Challenge
a. Insufficient class time to cover all the curriculum	①	②	③	④
b. Wide range of student abilities to address in class	①	②	③	④
c. Large class size	①	②	③	④
d. Inadequate resources (e.g., textbooks, equipment, teachers' aides)	①	②	③	④
e. Frequent changes in school priorities or leadership	①	②	③	④
f. Lack of planning time built into the school day	①	②	③	④
g. Lack of high-quality professional development opportunities for teachers	①	②	③	④
h. Complying with state and federal accountability requirements	①	②	③	④
i. Complying with union policies	①	②	③	④

19. **Please indicate the extent to which you agree or disagree with the following statements about you and your school. (Mark one number in each row.)**

	Strongly Disagree	Disagree	Agree	Strongly Agree
a. Our school has clearly defined goals for student learning.	①	②	③	④
b. Our school has clear strategies for improving teaching and learning.	①	②	③	④
c. Many new programs come and go in our school.	①	②	③	④
d. Most changes introduced at this school gain little support among teachers.	①	②	③	④
e. Many of the students I teach are so far behind grade level that they are not capable of learning the material I am supposed to teach them.	①	②	③	④
f. By trying different teaching methods, I can improve my students' achievement.	①	②	③	④
g. There is a great deal of cooperative effort among staff members.	①	②	③	④
h. Teachers in this school are continually learning and seeking new ideas.	①	②	③	④
i. With effort, all of my students can achieve at high levels.	①	②	③	④

20. **Think about the frequency with which leaders in your school have performed the following actions since the beginning of the school year.**

In the first set of columns, please indicate the frequency with which your <u>principal</u> has performed the following actions.
In the second set of columns, please indicate whether any <u>other school leaders</u> *regularly* lead or assist in these activities.

Since the beginning of the school year, my principal has...	Frequency of <u>principal</u> actions since beginning of school year (Mark one)				<u>Others</u> who *regularly* take these actions (Mark all that apply)		
	Never	A Few Times	Once or Twice a month	Once or Twice a Week or More	Assistant Principal	Coach	Other School Leader(s) (e.g., dept chair)
a. Given me useful feedback and/or suggestions on my teaching	①	②	③	④	○	○	○
b. Given me useful suggestions on how to integrate the Principles of Learning into my instructional practice	①	②	③	④	○	○	○
c. Conducted a Learning Walk in my classroom	①	②	③	④	○	○	○
d. Visited my classroom for more than 30 minutes (not a Learning Walk)	①	②	③	④	○	○	○
e. Provided feedback to the faculty on Learning Walks in my or other teachers' classrooms	①	②	③	④	○	○	○
f. Led professional development sessions in which I participated	①	②	③	④	○	○	○
g. Reviewed student work with me (individually or in a group)	①	②	③	④	○	○	○
h. Attended or participated in my grade level, team, or department meetings	①	②	③	④	○	○	○

21. Think about the <u>leadership your principal provides</u> at your school. Please indicate the extent to which you agree or disagree with each of the following statements about your principal's leadership? (Mark one number in each row.)

The principal at my school...	Strongly Disagree	Disagree	Agree	Strongly Agree	Don't Know
a. Sets high standards for teaching and learning	①	②	③	④	⓪
b. Has limited experience and/or knowledge of best instructional practices	①	②	③	④	⓪
c. Encourages teachers to review the Principles of Learning and integrate them into our classrooms	①	②	③	④	⓪
d. Helps us adapt our teaching practices according to analysis of state or district assessment results	①	②	③	④	⓪
e. Helps us understand and use the curriculum guide(s) to guide our teaching	①	②	③	④	⓪
f. Enforces school rules for student conduct and backs me up when needed	①	②	③	④	⓪
g. Spends too much time out of the school building	①	②	③	④	⓪
h. Has little time to regularly visit classrooms	①	②	③	④	⓪
i. Fills up my planning time with logistical and administrative items	①	②	③	④	⓪
j. Arranges for support when I need it (e.g., access to coaches, outside consultants, district curriculum staff)	①	②	③	④	⓪
k. Regularly attends professional development sessions in which I participate	①	②	③	④	⓪

22. Think about the <u>support provided by coaches</u> at your school. Please indicate the extent to which you agree or disagree with each of the following statements about your literacy and math coach. If you have more than one literacy or math coach, please refer to the coach that works closest with you. (Mark two numbers in each row.)

○ If you currently serve as a part-time math or literacy coach, go to Question 23.

	Literacy Coach					Math Coach				
	○ My school does not have a literacy coach ○ I do not teach literacy (skip this column if you marked one or both bubbles)					○ My school does not have a math coach ○ I do not teach math (skip this column if you marked one or both bubbles)				
My coach...	Strongly Disagree	Disagree	Agree	Strongly Agree	Don't Know	Strongly Disagree	Disagree	Agree	Strongly Agree	Don't Know
a. Has given me useful feedback and/or suggestions about my teaching	①	②	③	④	⓪	①	②	③	④	⓪
b. Is knowledgeable about content and pedagogy in his/her area of assignment	①	②	③	④	⓪	①	②	③	④	⓪
c. Has little time to support teachers	①	②	③	④	⓪	①	②	③	④	⓪
d. Has worked with me individually on a regular basis	①	②	③	④	⓪	①	②	③	④	⓪
e. Spends too much time out of the school building	①	②	③	④	⓪	①	②	③	④	⓪
f. Is someone I trust to help me and provide support when I need it	①	②	③	④	⓪	①	②	③	④	⓪
g. Is not as helpful at providing instructional advice as other teachers and/or administrators in my school	①	②	③	④	⓪	①	②	③	④	⓪
h. Clearly communicates messages from the principal and district	①	②	③	④	⓪	①	②	③	④	⓪
i. Has helped me to make important changes to my instructional practice	①	②	③	④	⓪	①	②	③	④	⓪

23. Please indicate the extent to which you agree or disagree with the following statements about your district. (Mark one number in each row.)

	Strongly Disagree	Disagree	Agree	Strongly Agree	Don't Know
a. District administrators communicate clear and consistent strategies for meeting student achievement goals.	①	②	③	④	⓪
b. It is difficult to implement the various district policies and reform initiatives because they often conflict with one another.	①	②	③	④	⓪
c. District administrators create mandates without providing adequate support.	①	②	③	④	⓪
d. District administrators visit and learn from school administration and staff.	①	②	③	④	⓪
e. District administrators do not understand the needs of our school.	①	②	③	④	⓪
f. District priorities are consistent with our school's priorities.	①	②	③	④	⓪

BACKGROUND

24. Including this year, how many years have you been a full-time teacher? (Fill in each space with zero or another number.)

a....in total?   **Years**   b....in this district?   **Years**   c....at this school?   **Years**

(columns of bubbles 0–9 for each)

25. What is your highest degree? (Mark one.)

○ a. Bachelor's Degree
○ b. Master's Degree
○ c. Doctorate Degree
○ d. Other (Specify_____)

26. What type of teaching certification do you hold? (Mark one.)

○ Not certified

○ Temporary, provisional, or emergency certification   ⇒ *These require additional coursework and/or student teaching before regular certification can be obtained.*

○ Regular, standard, or probationary* certification in *all* of the grade levels, subjects, and specialized areas (e.g., special education, ESL/bilingual) that you teach   ⇒ ** Probationary certification refers to initial certification issued after satisfying all requirements except the completion of a probationary period.*

○ Regular, standard, or probationary* certification in *some* of the grade levels, subjects, and specialized areas (e.g., special education, ESL/bilingual) that you teach

○ Regular, standard, or probationary* certification in *none* of the grade levels, subjects, and specialized areas (e.g., special education, ESL/bilingual) that you teach

Thank you very much for completing this survey.
Please place your completed survey in the envelope and send it to:
CPC Services
3975 Continental Drive
Columbia, PA 17512

PLEASE DO NOT WRITE IN THIS AREA

District Instructional Improvement Efforts:
PRINCIPAL SURVEY

RAND, an independent research organization with funding from the Hewlett Foundation, is conducting a study of instructional reform efforts of three urban school districts. The purpose of this survey is to obtain principals' views on instructional improvement efforts taking place within your school and district, and to assist your district and others in making improvements to these efforts. It's important that all individuals in your district participate in this survey so that results will fairly represent the opinions and experiences of principals in your district. Completing this survey is voluntary, but the information you provide will be critical for understanding the nature and impact of district reform efforts.

RAND will keep your responses strictly confidential. Once sealed into the reply envelope, no one at your school or district will see the completed survey. Results of the survey will be reported only in summary statistical form so that neither individuals nor their schools can be identified. We will not disclose your identity or information that identifies you to anyone outside the research project.

The survey should take approximately 20 minutes to complete. Please use a No. 2 pencil to fill out the survey. If you have any questions or concerns regarding this survey you can contact the person below for clarification. After you are finished, please mail your survey back in the envelope provided.

THANK YOU, in advance, for your time and input.

PLEASE DO NOT WRITE IN THIS AREA

1. **Please estimate the number of classroom teachers you have at your school in the following categories. (Fill in each space with zero or another number.)**

> *A "classroom teacher" includes teachers with direct responsibilities for teaching students, for example, teachers of academic and/or elective courses, special education teachers, resource teachers, and ESL/LEP teachers. This does not include teacher aides, student teachers, long- or short-term substitutes, paraprofessionals, full-time coaches, and other non-teaching professionals such as nurses or guidance counselors.*

a. Total number of classroom teachers

b. Teachers new to your school this year

c. Teachers who have been teaching for less than three years.

Number (Estimate)

2. **Please consider all of the <u>professional development</u> opportunities offered to teachers at your school this year, including any district, school, or externally provided trainings, workshops, and coaching activities.**

   To what extent were the following areas of professional development for teachers <u>a priority</u> at your school this year (including last summer)? (Mark one number in each row.)

	Not a Priority	Low Priority	Medium Priority	High Priority
a. Aligning curriculum and instruction with state and/or district content standards	①	②	③	④
b. Tailoring instructional strategies to special student populations [e.g., English as a second language (ESL) learners, students with IEPs]	①	②	③	④
c. Familiarizing students with state test format and test-taking strategies	①	②	③	④
d. Reviewing and implementing your school's improvement plan	①	②	③	④
e. Integrating the Principles of Learning into instructional practice	①	②	③	④
f. Implementing the district curriculum guides	①	②	③	④
g. Using student work to think about changing instruction or curricula	①	②	③	④
h. Interpreting and using reports of student test results to guide instruction	①	②	③	④

3. **Please indicate the extent to which you agree or disagree with the following statements about the curriculum guides in your district. (Mark one number in each row.)**

	Strongly Disagree	Disagree	Agree	Strongly Agree	Don't Know
a. The curriculum guides promote consistency of instruction <u>among classes</u> at the same grade level.	①	②	③	④	⓪
b. The curriculum guides promote continuity of instruction <u>between grades</u>.	①	②	③	④	⓪
c. It is unclear how the Principles of Learning are intended to support or fit in with the curriculum guides.	①	②	③	④	⓪
d. Curriculum guides have contributed to the improvement of the quality of instruction in my school.	①	②	③	④	⓪
e. Teachers express frustration with the curriculum guides (e.g., pacing, content, lack of flexibility).	①	②	③	④	⓪
f. The curriculum guides appropriately address the needs of special student populations [e.g., English as a second language (ESL) learners, students with IEPs].	①	②	③	④	⓪
g. The curriculum guides help prepare students at this school for the state tests.	①	②	③	④	⓪
h. The curriculum guides are too rigorous for most of the students at this school.	①	②	③	④	⓪
i. The curriculum guides help me better observe and give feedback to teachers.	①	②	③	④	⓪
j. There were opportunities for me and my teachers to provide feedback to the district about the curriculum guides during their development.	①	②	③	④	⓪

SCHOOL LEADERSHIP

4. The next question asks about your responsibilities as a school leader. In a <u>typical week</u>, how much time do you spend on the following areas/activities? In your opinion, how important are these tasks for being an effective school leader? (Mark one number for amount of time spent and one for importance in each row.)

	Amount of time spent in typical week				How important for being an effective school leader			
	No time (0 hours)	A small amount of time (1–4 hours)	A moderate amount of time (5–15 hours)	A lot of time (More than 15 hours)	Not Important	Somewhat Important	Moderately Important	Very Important
a. Overseeing management issues (e.g., budget issues, personnel, administrative paperwork)	①	②	③	④	①	②	③	④
b. Developing or leading professional development for staff (e.g., workshops, study groups)	①	②	③	④	①	②	③	④
c. Handling student discipline issues	①	②	③	④	①	②	③	④
d. Communicating with parents and the community	①	②	③	④	①	②	③	④
e. Visiting teachers' classrooms for more than 30 minutes at a time	①	②	③	④	①	②	③	④
f. Providing feedback and suggestions to teachers regarding curriculum and instruction	①	②	③	④	①	②	③	④
g. Giving teachers suggestions on how to integrate the Principles of Learning into their instructional practices	①	②	③	④	①	②	③	④
h. Reviewing student work with teachers	①	②	③	④	①	②	③	④
i. Reviewing student achievement data	①	②	③	④	①	②	③	④
j. Participating in your own professional development (e.g., attending workshops, study groups)	①	②	③	④	①	②	③	④

5. How many assistant principals do you have at your school? (Mark one.)

	Zero	One	Two	Three or more
Number of assistant principals	⓪	①	②	③

Questions 6-8 ask about district-sponsored activities to support your professional growth and development.

6. During the current school year (including last summer), how many times did you engage in each of the following _types_ of district-sponsored activities to support your professional growth and development? If you engaged in an activity, overall how valuable was each for your own professional development? (Mark one number for frequency and, if you engaged in the activity, one for value in each row.)

	Frequency of activity				Overall, value of activity for your professional development (if you engaged in an activity)			
	Never	Once or twice a year	Once or twice a month	At least once a week	Not Valuable	Minimally Valuable	Moderately Valuable	Very Valuable
a. Participating in a formal coaching or mentoring relationship with another principal	①	②	③	④	①	②	③	④
b. Attending district-sponsored principal seminars or meetings	①	②	③	④	①	②	③	④
c. Participating in Learning Walks conducted by district staff and/or other principals at your school	①	②	③	④	①	②	③	④
d. Participating in Learning Walks conducted by you and/or your staff members at your school	①	②	③	④	①	②	③	④
e. Participating in Learning Walks at other schools in the district	①	②	③	④	①	②	③	④
f. Discussing your work with your supervisor	①	②	③	④	①	②	③	④
g. Collaborating or sharing ideas with other principals	①	②	③	④	①	②	③	④

7. Now think about the <u>content</u> of district-sponsored activities to support your professional growth and development.

During your participation in professional development activities organized by the district this school year (including last summer), how much <u>emphasis</u> was placed on the following areas? If emphasized, how <u>useful</u> was the professional development received in each area for your practice as a school leader? (Mark one number for emphasis and, if emphasized, one for usefulness in each row.)

	Amount of emphasis in district-sponsored professional development activities				Usefulness of professional development *(if emphasized)*			
	No Emphasis	Minor Emphasis	Moderate Emphasis	Major Emphasis	Not Useful	Minimally Useful	Moderately Useful	Very Useful
a. Managing your school (e.g., budget, personnel, administrative issues)	①	②	③	④	①	②	③	④
b. Designing and implementing a school improvement plan	①	②	③	④	①	②	③	④
c. Understanding and helping teachers use state standards and assessments	①	②	③	④	①	②	③	④
d. Using curriculum guides to guide instruction	①	②	③	④	①	②	③	④
e. Using state and district assessment results to guide school improvement	①	②	③	④	①	②	③	④
f. Understanding and helping teachers use the Principles of Learning	①	②	③	④	①	②	③	④
g. Learning lessons from other schools	①	②	③	④	①	②	③	④
h. Understanding proper implementation of district, state, and federal policies and procedures (e.g., accountability, attendance, student promotion)	①	②	③	④	①	②	③	④

8. **Over the past few years, many of the professional development opportunities organized by the district for principals have been associated with the Institute for Learning (IFL) (e.g., Learning Walks, seminars on Principles of Learning or Disciplinary Literacy). Please indicate the extent to which you agree or disagree with the following statements about the overall impact of IFL-related professional development opportunities. (Mark one number in each row.)**

○ **If you have not participated in professional development activities associated with the Institute for Learning, please mark here and skip to Question 9.**

Overall, IFL-related professional development opportunities have. . .	Strongly Disagree	Disagree	Agree	Strongly Agree	Don't Know
a. Deepened my understanding of how children and adults learn	①	②	③	④	⓪
b. Added nothing new to what I already know about good instructional practice	①	②	③	④	⓪
c. Helped me better comment on and provide feedback to teachers' classroom instruction	①	②	③	④	⓪
d. Helped me identify teachers needing assistance	①	②	③	④	⓪
e. Failed to provide ideas that are relevant to my school	①	②	③	④	⓪
f. Helped me design higher quality professional development for teachers	①	②	③	④	⓪
g. Provided principals in the district a "common language" facilitating dialogue and collaboration	①	②	③	④	⓪
h. Had a greater impact on me in previous years than in recent years	①	②	③	④	⓪

9. **During the current school year (2003-04) and last school year (2002-03), were you formally evaluated as a principal? (Mark all that apply.)**

○ Yes, I was evaluated or am in the process of being evaluated this year (e.g., had initial goal-setting meeting in 2003-04)
○ Yes, I was evaluated in 2002-03
○ No ➡ SKIP TO QUESTION 11

10. **Please indicate the extent to which you agree or disagree with the following statements about the <u>most current principal evaluation process</u> in which you participated in your district. (Mark one number in each row.)**

	Strongly Disagree	Disagree	Agree	Strongly Agree
a. The evaluation process helps me identify my strengths and weaknesses.	①	②	③	④
b. The evaluation process is an exercise that carries no consequences.	①	②	③	④
c. My evaluator has been constructive and supportive.	①	②	③	④
d. I know what is expected of me and how my performance is evaluated.	①	②	③	④
e. My evaluator provides me with feedback (in a written or oral format).	①	②	③	④
f. My evaluator follows up with me on areas of weakness identified in my evaluation.	①	②	③	④
g. I receive training or support from the district to improve on areas of weakness identified in my evaluation.	①	②	③	④
h. My evaluator is knowledgeable about my school's context (e.g., issues relevant to my school's grade level, student characteristics).	①	②	③	④

11. **Please indicate the extent to which you agree or disagree with the following statements about <u>interactions with your primary supervisor</u>. (Mark one number in each row.)**

My supervisor. . .

	Strongly Disagree	Disagree	Agree	Strongly Agree
a. Provides useful suggestions on how to be an effective school leader	①	②	③	④
b. Does not visit my school often enough to understand and help meet my schools' needs	①	②	③	④
c. Is knowledgeable about education at this level of schooling	①	②	③	④
d. Lacks up-to-date knowledge about the most current instructional theories and practices	①	②	③	④
e. Regularly monitors my activities to ensure that I am helping teachers with major district efforts (e.g., curriculum guides, Principles of Learning)	①	②	③	④
f. Is someone I trust to help me and provide support when I need it	①	②	③	④

USE OF DATA FOR PLANNING AND DECISION MAKING

12. Were the following sources of information available to you? If so, overall how useful was each source to you and/or your leadership team **for making decisions about instructional matters** at your school? (Mark one number in each row.)

	Not Available	Not Useful	Available and... Minimally Useful	Moderately Useful	Very Useful
a. School-wide student performance results on state test(s)	①	②	③	④	⑤
b. Student performance results on state test(s) disaggregated by student groups (e.g., grade level, classrooms, student characteristics)	①	②	③	④	⑤
c. Student performance results on state test(s) disaggregated by subtopic or skill	①	②	③	④	⑤
d. Student performance on district assessments	①	②	③	④	⑤
e. Surveys of teachers	①	②	③	④	⑤
f. Retention and dropout data	①	②	③	④	⑤
g. Attendance and mobility rates	①	②	③	④	⑤
h. Information gained through Learning Walk(s) at your school	①	②	③	④	⑤
i. Results of systematic review(s) of student work	①	②	③	④	⑤

13. Please indicate the extent to which you agree or disagree with the following statements about **your district's role** in supporting data use for school decision making and planning. (Mark one number in each row.)

Our district...	Strongly Disagree	Disagree	Agree	Strongly Agree	Don't Know
a. Provides useful *reports & presentations* of student achievement data	①	②	③	④	⓪
b. Provides useful *assistance* in analyzing student achievement data	①	②	③	④	⓪
c. Is responsive when I have specific questions about student achievement data	①	②	③	④	⓪
d. Provides useful assistance in identifying research-based improvement strategies	①	②	③	④	⓪
e. Is better at diagnosing school problems than finding solutions	①	②	③	④	⓪

14. Please indicate the extent to which you agree or disagree with the following statements about your current <u>school improvement plan</u> and the <u>planning process</u> undertaken to develop that plan. (Mark one number in each row.)

	Strongly Disagree	Disagree	Agree	Strongly Agree	Don't Know
a. The school improvement planning process was an important process for my school to undergo.	①	②	③	④	⓪
b. The school improvement planning process was more labor intensive than it needs to be.	①	②	③	④	⓪
c. The district did not provide enough support and information to undertake the school improvement planning process.	①	②	③	④	⓪
d. The district monitors the degree to which our school improvement plan has been implemented.	①	②	③	④	⓪
e. The school improvement plan guides decisions about *professional development* in this school.	①	②	③	④	⓪
f. The school improvement plan guides decisions about the *allocation of resources to support instruction* (e.g., time, materials) in this school.	①	②	③	④	⓪
g. The school improvement plan guides decisions about *instructional strategies* (e.g., curriculum choices, teaching methods) in this school.	①	②	③	④	⓪
h. The school improvement plan guides decisions about *organizational structures that support instruction* (e.g., class size, student assignment) in this school.	①	②	③	④	⓪
i. The school improvement plan is something that we only use to comply with district or state requirements.	①	②	③	④	⓪
j. The district provides clear and consistent guidance for the development of our school improvement plan.	①	②	③	④	⓪
k. I have observed positive changes in the *quality of teaching* as a result of implementing strategies contained in our school improvement plan.	①	②	③	④	⓪

15. Which of the following characterizes your school? (Mark one answer in each row.)

	Yes	No	Don't Know	
a. My school met <u>all</u> **Adequate Yearly Progress (AYP) requirements** for the 2002-03 school year.	○	○	○	➡ *"Adequate yearly progress" is the amount of yearly improvement each school is expected to make under state accountability provisions.*
b. My school was identified as **"in need of improvement"** by the state in 2002-03.	○	○	○	➡ *Schools that fail to make adequate yearly progress, as defined by their state, for two consecutive years, are identified as "in need of improvement" under federal accountability provisions.*

SCHOOL CONTEXT AND BACKGROUND

16. **Please indicate the extent to which you agree or disagree with the following statements about your <u>district</u>. (Mark one number in each row.)**

	Strongly Disagree	Disagree	Agree	Strongly Agree	Don't Know
a. District administrators communicate clear and consistent strategies for meeting student achievement goals.	①	②	③	④	⓪
b. It is difficult to implement the various district policies and reform initiatives because they often conflict with one another.	①	②	③	④	⓪
c. District administrators distribute resources fairly throughout the district.	①	②	③	④	⓪
d. District administrators create mandates without providing adequate support.	①	②	③	④	⓪
e. When schools are having difficulty, district staff provide assistance to help them improve.	①	②	③	④	⓪
f. District administrators visit and learn from school administration and staff.	①	②	③	④	⓪
g. District administrators do not understand the needs of our school.	①	②	③	④	⓪
h. District priorities are consistent with our school's priorities.	①	②	③	④	⓪
i. District administrators provide little to no follow-up on the professional development activities organized for principals.	①	②	③	④	⓪
j. District administrators and staff (e.g., supervisors, curriculum/instructional staff) provide useful assistance and consultation to support me and my school.	①	②	③	④	⓪

17. **To what extent is each of the following a challenge to your efforts to improve teaching and learning in your school? (Mark one number in each row.)**

	Not a Challenge	A Minor Challenge	A Moderate Challenge	A Great Challenge
a. Teacher turnover	①	②	③	④
b. Shortage of highly qualified teachers	①	②	③	④
c. Complying with state and federal accountability requirements	①	②	③	④
d. Complying with union policies	①	②	③	④
e. Inadequate time to prepare before implementing new reforms	①	②	③	④
f. Lack of high-quality professional development opportunities <u>for teachers</u>	①	②	③	④
g. Lack of high-quality professional development opportunities for <u>principals</u>	①	②	③	④
h. Instability of funding from year to year	①	②	③	④
i. Frequent changes in district policy and reform priorities	①	②	③	④
j. Frequent changes in district leadership	①	②	③	④

18. Please indicate the number of years you have worked in the field of education in this school or in other schools. (Fill in each space with zero or another number.)

a. Principal

Number of years at THIS school	Number of years at OTHER schools in THIS district	Number of years at schools OUTSIDE THIS district

b. Other positions (e.g., teacher, administrator, instructional specialist)

Number of years at THIS school	Number of years at OTHER schools in THIS district (or at the central office)	Number of years at schools OUTSIDE THIS district

19. What year did you receive your administrative credential? (Fill in year or mark circle.)

○ I still have not received my credential

YEAR

20. Over the past five years, how many principals (including yourself) has your school had? (Fill in number or mark circle.)

○ Don't know

Number of principals

21. Please use this space for additional comments about your role as principal or your district's instructional improvement efforts.

Thank you very much for completing this survey. Please place your completed survey in the envelope and send it to:

CPC Services
3975 Continental Drive
Columbia, PA 17512

PLEASE DO NOT WRITE IN THIS AREA

Technical Notes on Research Methods

Case Study School Selection

Team members visited case study schools in each district to gather detailed information on district initiatives from school personnel. Table B.1 shows the number of schools at each level visited in the three districts in both years of data collection. Our resources allowed us to visit 16 schools in year 1 and 17 schools in year 2 in Monroe, ten schools in each year in Roosevelt, and nine schools in year 1 and ten schools in year 2 in Jefferson. In general, we selected schools to represent the variation that existed across each district, including grade level served, student demographic characteristics, school performance level, and other district-specific school reforms (e.g., schools targeted by specific initiatives).

Table B.1
Breakdown of Schools by Year of Data Collection

	Elementary Schools		Middle Schools		High Schools	
	Year 1	Year 2	Year 1	Year 2	Year 1	Year 2
Monroe	7	9	5	4	4	4
Roosevelt	6	4	1	3	3	3
Jefferson	5	6	2	2	2	2

Across all three districts, the purpose and structure of the visits changed from year 1 to year 2. In year 1, researchers spent less time on site in each district and focused on broad questions, getting an overview of district initiatives and their implementation at the school level. In year 2, researchers spent more days on site in each district and used targeted, detailed questions, building on data collected in the first year to gain a deeper understanding of the implementation and impact of district initiatives.

Survey Methods

Sampling Methods (Monroe Teachers)

We designed surveys to be administered to a census of all teachers and all principals in each district. However, to limit the burden placed on teachers, district leaders in Monroe asked us to reduce the number of teachers surveyed. Therefore, we created a sampling framework that included teachers from a subset of schools in Monroe. Within this subset of schools, we included a sample of teachers in larger schools and all teachers in smaller schools. Table B.2 details the strata we used to select schools in Monroe, based on three critical variables: grade level, student performance, and, in the case of low-performing schools, level of support from the district (a subset of low-performing schools had been targeted by district leaders for specific interventions). We based student performance strata on state-defined school performance levels, which the state determined

Table B.2
Outline of Strata Used to Create Survey Sampling Framework, Monroe

Performance	Low With Support	Low Without Support	Middle	High
Elementary				
Middle				
High				

using multiple indicators (e.g., student achievement on core subject tests, school dropout rates).

Ultimately, we collapsed the middle and high performance categories because of the small number of schools that fell into these categories. Negotiations with the district resulted in a sample that included all the schools in the "low with support" category, all middle and high schools, and a random selection of half of the elementary schools in the "low without support" and "middle/high" performance categories. As Table B.3 shows, the final school survey sample included 72 schools: 44 elementary schools, 17 middle schools, and 11 high schools. Statistical comparisons between sample and non-sample elementary schools showed no significant differences between the two groups.[1]

To collect sufficient data to create reliable school-level measures, we sought 30 teacher respondents from each school. Assuming a 70-percent response rate, we determined that 43 teachers should be sampled in each school. Based on this calculation, all teachers in schools with 43 or fewer teachers were surveyed, and a random sample of 43 teachers was surveyed in schools that had more than 43 classroom teachers. In schools where a random sample of teachers was drawn, sampling was performed by the district.

Table B.3
Survey Sample of Schools Versus Total Number, Monroe

	Low With Support		Low Without Support		Middle		High	
	Sample	Total No.	Sample	Total No.	Sample	Total No.	Sample	Total No.
Elementary	12	12	10	20	14	27	8	15
Middle	7	7	8	8	2	2	0	0
High	5	5	4	4	0	0	2	2
Total	23	23	22	33	16	29	10	17

---

[1] The following variables were used to compare sample and non-sample elementary schools: combined test scores for grade 3 and 4 math and reading, percentage of economically disadvantaged students, percentage of LEP students, percentage White, percentage Hispanic, and the number of students.

Survey Administration

The research team developed teacher and principal surveys that included questions on the following topics: professional development; availability and use of data; district curriculum guidance; instructional leadership; supervision of principals; school improvement plans; school and district context; and respondent background. Our subcontractor, Pearson NCS, developed machine scannable versions of the surveys and handled most administrative and processing services. District-specific versions of both surveys were created that included similar questions with slight changes in wording to reflect district terminology and program names. Before survey administration, we piloted the surveys with a small number of teachers and principals in each district. Each pilot participant completed the survey and participated in a follow-up interview to discuss specific survey questions and provide input on possible revision of survey items. Pilot participants received an honorarium of $50. We revised surveys based on feedback from the pilot testing. After the surveys were finalized, Pearson NCS mailed them to teachers and principals at their school addresses starting in March 2004. Survey administration time frames varied slightly across districts to reflect state testing calendars; the mailing dates ensured that surveys did not arrive during or immediately before administration of state assessments.

The instructions mailed with the surveys asked teachers and principals to complete their surveys and return them in a postage-paid return envelope. Pearson NCS sent postcards shortly after the first mailing to remind recipients to complete and return their surveys. We sent those who did not complete the survey within a specified time period another copy of the survey. We sent a third mailing to teachers and principals in Jefferson and Roosevelt who did not complete either of the first two surveys; because of an earlier end to the school year, Monroe teachers did not receive a third survey mailing. Overall, teachers had multiple opportunities to respond to the survey over a period of three months.

We made several efforts to encourage higher response rates. First, the survey was accompanied by a letter from the district superintendent encouraging teacher and principal participation. In Jefferson and Roosevelt, we also created school-level incentives for survey completion. Schools where 60 percent or more of the teachers completed and returned the survey received $100 and schools where 80 percent or more completed and returned the survey received $200. The incentives in Monroe were slightly different because not all teachers in the district were surveyed. In Monroe, principals received $10 gift cards and teachers received 30-minute pre-paid phone cards with the first survey mailing. Additionally, the Survey Research Group at RAND called all schools in each district, encouraging principals to return their surveys and to remind teachers in their schools to complete their surveys. In the latter stages of the survey administration, these calls targeted schools with especially low teacher response rates. Finally, reminder fliers were sent to teachers and principals in all three districts to encourage participation in the survey. Pearson NCS processed all completed surveys and provided RAND researchers with final data files and tracking information on numbers of surveys completed by school and district.

In the end, we received lower-than-expected response rates on the teacher surveys (see Table 2.3), limiting our ability to construct school-level estimates, as we had hoped to do. We did, however, create district-level estimates for all teachers using weighted survey results (see description below). We investigated a few hypotheses to explain the lower-than-expected response rates (e.g., union resistance, other competing surveys), but we could not verify any significant explanation. Although the low response rates obviously limit the ability to generalize to all teachers in each district, the weights described below minimize the potential nonresponse bias.

Weights

Construction of the teacher weights occurred in two steps. First, to account for the sampling scheme that was implemented for teachers in Monroe, we created survey sampling weights for each teacher. This allowed us to use the sample to reflect the population of teachers from which it was drawn. Second, to adjust for nonresponse bias that often occurs when using survey data, we constructed nonresponse weights. Nonresponse bias occurs when a systematic difference occurs between survey responders and nonresponders.

The development of the sampling weights for the Monroe school district also occurred in two steps, mirroring the selection process itself. (We constructed the weights for the sampling of teachers after we created the weights for the sampling of schools.)

As mentioned in the previous section, we based the sampling of schools from the Monroe school district on six strata (middle and high schools, and elementary schools by the four performance rating categories). Since we included in the sample all district middle and high schools, they received a school weight equal to 1. The same was true for elementary schools with a low performance rating with support. The other three types of elementary schools received school weights equal to the inverse of the proportion of schools sampled.

For the teachers, the probability of being sampled from an individual school was based on the total number of teachers at the school. The teacher component of the sampling weight was equal to the inverse of the number of teachers sampled divided by the total number of teachers in the school (recall that in schools with more than 43 teachers, only 43 teachers were included in the sample).

The teacher sampling weight was based on the probability of the school being sampled as well as the probability of the teacher being sampled from the school's teacher population. Therefore, the final sampling weight was obtained by multiplying the school sampling weight by the teacher sampling weight.

Whereas teacher sampling weights needed to be applied only for Monroe teachers, nonresponse weights were created for teachers in all three districts. To determine whether weighting for nonresponse was necessary, we looked at variables that may have been different between those who responded to the survey and those who failed to respond. Variables that we further examined included the number of years of teaching experience, teacher certification status, school level, and whether the teacher was a math or English teacher (for high school teachers only). For each district, we performed t-tests to check for statistically significant differences between responders and nonresponders. These tests showed significant differences between responders and nonresponders along each of these variables, with the exception of high school subject taught.[2] This implied that a nonresponse bias existed. To reduce this bias, we calculated nonresponse weights from a logistic regression where response status was the dependent variable. The independent variables included school level, teacher certification status, number of years of teaching experience, percentage of students from low-income families and percentage of nonwhite students. In addition, we used a district-specific rating for school performance status. The nonresponse weight for each teacher was calculated as the inverse of the predicted value obtained from each district's logistic model. While there are obviously other potential reasons for nonresponse, we did our best to identify those variables for which we had reliable data and that we would expect to influence how teachers might respond to the specific questions asked on the survey.

By multiplying the sampling weight and the nonresponse weight together, we combined both parts of the weighting process to obtain a final weight for each teacher. Then we developed a scale factor (the number of observations divided by the sum of the weights). Multiplying by this factor scaled the final weights. On further inspection, none of the weights was deemed extreme. We then applied the final weight to the calculation of all teacher survey results presented in this report.

Finally, in all three districts, we included all principals in the survey sample. Therefore, sampling weights did not need to be applied. Because the response rates were considered to be sufficiently

---

[2] At the time that we needed to make decisions about nonresponders, we had data for only two of the three districts (Monroe and Jefferson). With respect to certification status, tests showed a significant difference in response rate for one of those districts and not the other. We decided not to control for certification in our nonresponse models because our sample had few uncertified teachers—i.e., it showed very little variation. Teachers with more experience and elementary and middle school teachers were more likely to respond in Monroe; in Jefferson, elementary teachers responded more than middle and high school teachers. Although these differences existed across districts, we controlled for the same variables in each district and we ran district-specific models to develop nonresponse weights.

high (approximately 70–80 percent in each district), we decided that weighting to reduce bias between responders and nonresponders was not necessary. In each case, the group of nonresponding principals was too small to provide statistically meaningful comparisons.

Student Achievement Trends

As part of our contextual description of the three study districts, we provide a depiction of student achievement trends in Tables C.1, C.2, and C.3. These tables are not meant to be a causal analysis relating student achievement to particular district reform efforts or to district partnerships with the IFL. Rather, they provide an overview of performance patterns from the 1997–98 through 2003–04 school years. The 1997–98 school year was chosen as a starting point because it precedes the time point when each district entered into a partnership with the IFL. Therefore, although changes in student achievement cannot be attributed to the district-IFL partnership, these analyses nonetheless provide a picture of the overall trend in student performance in the study districts over the course of time when they were engaged in the partnership up to the end of this study.

This appendix presents two types of achievement trends. First, we examine district trends over time in the percentage of students reaching proficiency and the percentage of low-performing students on state assessment tests. We then compare district performance on state assessments to the average performance in the state in which each district is situated to assess whether there was a difference in achievement between each district and its state and the degree to which that difference narrowed or widened over time.

Table C.1 depicts the progress each district has made in increasing the percentage of students reaching proficiency and reducing the percentage of low-performing students in reading/ELA and math

Table C.1

District Changes in Percentages of Proficient and Low-Performing Students, 1997–98 through 2003–04

	Monroe					
	Grade 4		Grade 8		Grade 10	
	Reading	Math	Reading	Math	ELA	Math
Average yearly gain in percentage proficient, 1997–98 through 2001–02	1.0	3.2	3.0	3.9	1.0	3.0
One-year gain in percentage proficient, 2002–03 through 2003–04	4.0	10.0	7.0	2.0	6.0	2.0

	Roosevelt					
	Grade 4		Grade 8		Grade 10	
	ELA	Math	ELA	Math	ELA	Math
Average yearly gain in percentage proficient	2.9	2.8	–2.9	–0.5	2.5	–2.7
Average yearly change in percentage of low-performing students	0.1	–0.1	1.0	–0.2	0.1	–2.2

	Jefferson					
	Grade 4		Grades 7/8		Grade 10	
	ELA	Math	ELA	Math	ELA	Math
Average yearly gain in percentage proficient	2.7	1.8	4.0	0.0	3.7	3.0
Average yearly change in percentage of low-performing students	–1.7	–2.5	–3.7	–1.0	–4.2	–6.3

NOTES: The state in which Monroe is situated instituted a new accountability test in the 2002–03 school year, forcing us to examine trends for two time frames: from 1997–98 through 2001–02 and from 2002–03 through 2003–04. In Roosevelt, the tenth grade average yearly gains and changes for ELA are based on the years 1998–99 through 2002–03 because of missing data and inconsistent testing; no test score data are available for 1997–98 and the state no longer tested tenth graders in 2003–04. For

Table C.1—continued

math, the gains and changes are based on the 1997–98 through 2002–03 school years because the state did not test tenth graders in 2003–04. Gains and changes for Jefferson are reported for seventh grade ELA and eighth grade math. The state in which Jefferson is situated changed from testing eighth graders in ELA to seventh graders in the 2000–01 school year. Due to the change in grades tested, Jefferson's gains and changes for seventh grade ELA are calculated from 2000–02 through 2003–04. In addition, the state made significant changes to the content of the fourth grade ELA assessment; therefore gains and changes for fourth grade ELA in Jefferson are also calculated from 2000–01 to 2003–04.

for grades 4, 8, and 10.[1] We analyze progress by calculating average yearly gains/changes, or the change in the percentage of students with the given performance level each year, averaged across years. For all rows representing gains in percentage proficient, a positive value indicates an increase in the percentage of proficient students, whereas a negative value indicates a decrease in the percentage proficient. Conversely, for all rows showing a change in percentage of low-performing students, a negative value indicates a reduction in the percentage of low-performing students and a positive value indicates an increase in the percentage of low-performing students.

Thus, improved student performance is indicated by positive values for gains in percentage proficient and negative values for change in percentage of low-performing students. For example, as Table C.1 indicates, in eighth grade reading/ELA, Jefferson demonstrated two indicators of improved student performance: a 4 percent average yearly gain in the percentage of students at the proficient level and a 3.7 percent average yearly decrease in the percentage of low-performing students.

In general, the table indicates that both Monroe and Jefferson made significant progress in increasing the percentage of proficient students across subject areas and grade levels, whereas Roosevelt made

---

[1] Definitions of low-performing students differed in the states in which Roosevelt and Jefferson are situated, but in both cases the category represents students in the lowest-scoring group. The state in which Monroe is situated reports fewer performance categories, so the percentage of low-performing students is simply the inverse of the percentage proficient. Therefore, we have excluded Monroe from analyses of the percentage of low-performing students. See notes for Table 3.b for details about years in which consistent test data are not available.

more-limited progress. With the exception of eighth grade math in Jefferson, where there was neither a gain nor a loss in the percentage of proficient students, both Monroe and Jefferson had positive yearly gains in the percentage of students reaching proficiency in both subject areas and for all three grade levels. The largest gains were seen in Monroe for the period from 2002–03 to 2003–04 after the implementation of a new state assessment. Roosevelt showed positive gains in the percentage proficient for both subject areas in fourth grade and also for tenth grade ELA. However, on average, Roosevelt's percentage of proficient students decreased on tenth grade math assessments and on assessments in both math and ELA for eighth graders over this period.

In terms of reducing the percentage of low-performing students, again, Jefferson made substantial progress while Roosevelt had more limited success. In each subject area and grade level, on average, Jefferson reduced the percentage of low-performing students. The greatest reductions were seen for tenth graders in both ELA and math. Jefferson's percentage of tenth graders categorized as low performing in math went from 72 percent in 1997–98 to 34 percent in 2003–04. Roosevelt showed minor reductions in the percentage of low-performing students in math at all three grade levels; however, the percentage of low-performing students increased slightly on average on ELA assessments at each tested grade level. Because the state in which Monroe is situated reports fewer performance categories, the percentage of low-performing students is simply the inverse of the percentage proficient. Therefore, Monroe was excluded from our analyses of changes in the percentage of low-performing students.

Tables C.2 and C.3 also show progress measured by increases in the percentage of proficient students and decreases in the percentage of low-performing students, but progress is now compared to the relative increases and decreases in each respective state. As in Table C.1, this analysis examines the trends in student achievement for the 1997–98 through 2003–04 school years. However, as in the previous table, the analysis is often truncated due to missing data or changes in tests. It should also be noted that while Monroe is included in Table

C.2, it is not included in Table C.3 because the state does not have an equivalent measure for low-performing students.

In both Tables C.2 and C.3, the difference between the state and district percentage of students scoring at each performance level is given for each year. For Table C.2, a negative value for a particular year indicates that the district had a lower percentage of proficient students than did the state, whereas a negative value in Table C.3 indicates that the district had a higher percentage of low-performing students. For each table, the last column displays the net change in the gap between district and state average percentage proficient and percentage low-performing students over time. This gain or loss is calculated as the difference between the initial gap in percentage proficient or low-performing students and gaps in the last observed year, based on the initial and final years in which we have consistent test data.[2] For both tables, a positive net change indicates improved student performance on the part of the district relative to the state, as measured by a closing of the gap between district and state performance over the time period shown.

As both tables highlight, the three study districts had a lower percentage of proficient students and a higher percentage of low-performing students than each of their respective states—overall for each subject and grade level and across all years. However, the values in the "Net Change" column also suggest that, in some cases, the districts made progress in closing the gap. As illustrated in Table C.2, of the three districts, Monroe had the smallest relative gap in percentage proficient between district and state in all years and made the most significant progress in closing the existing gaps. In both reading and math for fourth and eighth graders, Monroe reduced the percentage proficient gap; it experienced only a minor widening of the gap for tenth graders in both subject areas.

Table C.2 also shows that Roosevelt and Jefferson both had significantly lower percentages of proficient students across each grade

---

[2] See notes to Table C.3 for details about years for which consistent test data are not available.

Table C.2
Difference Between State and District Averages on the Percentage Scoring Proficient in ELA and Mathematics, 1997–98 to 2003–04

	1997–98	1998–99	1999–00	2000–01	2001–02	2002–03	2003–04	Net Change in Gap Between State and District Averages
Grade 4								
Monroe								
Reading	-3.5	-5.4	-2.7	-1.6	-2.3	NA	NA	1.2
Mathematics	-7.5	-9.4	-5.5	-3.1	-2.8	NA	NA	4.7
Roosevelt								
ELA	-21.8	-24.3	-20.8	-25.0	-26.2	-24.7	-21.4	0.4
Mathematics	-18.7	-23.3	-20.0	-21.7	-25.0	-23.3	-23.3	-4.6
Jefferson								
ELA	NA	NA	NA	-23.0	-23.0	-23.0	-20.0	3.0
Mathematics	-19.0	-20.0	-21.0	-19.0	-20.0	-19.0	-16.0	3.0
Grades 7/8								
Monroe								
Reading	-8.0	-9.7	-8.2	-8.0	-5.2	NA	NA	2.8
Mathematics	-13.5	-13.9	-10.1	-8.4	-7.0	NA	NA	6.5
Roosevelt								
Reading	-17.8	-21.6	-19.5	-22.0	-24.0	-22.8	-23.6	-5.8
Mathematics	-16.3	-19.0	-20.3	-20.0	-24.0	-23.5	-26.3	-10.0
Jefferson								
ELA	NA	NA	NA	-32.0	-32.0	-35.0	-33.0	-1.0
Mathematics	-22.0	-23.0	-27.0	-25.0	-28.0	-30.0	-30.0	-8.0

Table C.2—continued

	1997–98	1998–99	1999–00	2000–01	2001–02	2002–03	2003–04	Net Change in Gap Between State and District Averages
Grade 10								
Monroe								
ELA	-1.9	-4.4	-2.6	-4.6	-4.1	NA	NA	-2.2
Mathematics	-6.0	-7.7	-5.1	-7.5	-7.8	NA	NA	-1.8
Roosevelt								
ELA	NA	-8.7	-16.8	-15.5	-20.4	-18.9	NA	-10.2
Mathematics	NA	-11.0	-10.3	-12.0	-12.3	-19.2	NA	-8.2
Jefferson								
ELA	-27.0	-22.0	-23.0	-22.0	-35.0	-31.0	-30.0	-3.0
Mathematics	-19.0	-19.0	-33.0	-34.0	-32.0	-33.0	-34.0	-15.0

NOTES: NA indicates either that the test score is not available for that particular year or that the accountability test is inconsistent with other years. Thus, the 2002–03 and 2003–04 school years were excluded from our Monroe analysis; the 1997–98 and 2003–04 school years were excluded from our Roosevelt tenth grade analysis; and the 1997–98 through 1999–00 school years were excluded from our Jefferson fourth and seventh grade analyses.

Table C.3
Difference Between State and District Averages on the Percentage of Low-Performing Students in ELA and Mathematics, 1997–98 to 2003–04

	1997–98	1998–99	1999–00	2000–01	2001–02	2002–03	2003–04	Net Change in Gap Between State and District Averages
Grade 4								
Roosevelt								
ELA	-0.8	-1.0	-0.5	-0.5	-1.0	-0.6	-0.8	0.0
Mathematics	-4.3	-10.0	-7.7	-6.0	-4.5	-5.0	-2.9	1.4
Jefferson								
ELA	NA	NA	NA	-12.0	-12.0	-12.0	-12.0	0.0
Mathematics	-19.0	-20.0	-20.0	-19.0	-19.0	-18.0	-13.0	6.0
Grades 7/8								
Roosevelt								
Reading	-0.3	-2.3	-0.8	-1.3	-1.3	-3.2	-1.4	-1.1
Mathematics	-18.3	-22.0	-13.0	-7.3	-19.0	-18.6	-17.8	0.5
Jefferson								
ELA	NA	NA	NA	-21.0	-19.0	-15.0	-15.0	6.0
Mathematics	-31.0	-34.0	-36.0	-35.0	-35.0	-36.0	-37.0	-6.0

Table C.3—continued

	1997–98	1998–99	1999–00	2000–01	2001–02	2002–03	2003–04	Net Change in Gap Between State and District Averages
Grade 10								
Roosevelt								
ELA	NA	–0.6	–0.5	–1.0	–1.3	–1.0	NA	–0.4
Mathematics	–11.7	–12.0	–8.0	–12.7	–11.7	–9.7	NA	2.0
Jefferson								
ELA	–23.0	–16.0	–13.0	–25.0	–28.0	–18.0	–15.0	8.0
Mathematics	–22.0	–14.0	–19.0	–34.0	–36.0	–27.0	–20.0	2.0

NOTES: NA indicates either that the test score is not available for that particular year or that the accountability test is inconsistent with other years. Thus, the 2002–03 and 2003–04 school years were excluded from our Monroe analysis; the 1997–98 and 2003–04 school years were excluded from our Roosevelt tenth grade analysis; and the 1997–98 through 1999–00 school years were excluded from our Jefferson fourth and seventh grade analyses.

level and subject area than did their respective states and had more limited success in closing the gap. At the elementary level, Jefferson reduced the gap between district and state proficiency levels in both ELA and math, but the gap widened in seventh grade ELA, eighth grade math, and tenth grade ELA and math. While showing a minor improvement in fourth grade ELA percentage proficient, Roosevelt saw a widening of the gap between district and state averages over time in all other grade levels and subject areas.

Although both Roosevelt and Jefferson have struggled in recent years to reach average state proficiency levels in several areas, the results displayed in Table C.3 show that both districts had some success maintaining or reducing the gap between district and state averages for the percentage of low-performing students. Again, both districts performed worse than the state as a whole on these performance measures, with greater percentages of low-performing students across all years, subject areas, and grade levels. However, Roosevelt gained on the state average over time in math performance across all three grade levels and remained stable or had only a slight widening of the gap across grades for ELA. Jefferson also succeeded in closing the gap between district and state averages for fourth and tenth graders in both ELA and math and seventh grade ELA, whereas in eighth grade math Jefferson lost ground compared with the state.

In total, these tables suggest that the three districts had some success in improving the performance of their students over the time during which they partnered with the IFL, with Monroe showing the greatest success. However, to examine the impact of district reform efforts in general or of the partnership with the IFL on student achievement, detailed student-level data of individual performance over time would be required. The data available for this study do not support such an analysis.

Principles of Learning

Organizing for Effort
Everything within the school is organized to support the belief that sustained and directed effort can yield high achievement for all students. High standards are set, and all students are given as much time and expert instruction as they need to meet or exceed the expectations.

Clear Expectations
Clear standards of achievement and gauges of students' progress toward those standards offer real incentives for students to work hard and succeed. Descriptive criteria and models that meet the standards are displayed in the schools, and the students refer to these displays to help them analyze and discuss their work.

Fair and Credible Evaluations
Tests, exams, and classroom assessments must be aligned to the standards of achievement for these assessments to be fair. Further, grading must be done against absolute standards rather than on a curve so that students can clearly see the results of their learning efforts.

Recognition of Accomplishment
Clear recognition of authentic student accomplishments is a hallmark of an effort-based school. Progress points are articulated so that, regardless of entering performance level, every student can meet the criteria for accomplishments often enough to be recognized frequently.

Academic Rigor in a Thinking Curriculum

In every subject, at every grade level, instruction and learning must include commitment to a knowledge core, high thinking demand, and active use of knowledge.

Accountable Talk[SM]

Accountable Talk means using evidence that is appropriate to the discipline and that follows established norms of good reasoning. Teachers should create the norms and skills of Accountable Talk in their classrooms.

Socializing Intelligence

Intelligence comprises problem solving and reasoning capabilities along with habits of mind that lead one to use those capabilities regularly. Equally, it is a set of beliefs about one's right and obligation to make sense of the world, and one's capacity to figure things out over time. By calling on students to use the skills of intelligent thinking—and by holding them responsible for doing so—educators can "teach" intelligence.

Self-Management of Learning

Students manage their own learning by evaluating feedback they get from others; by bringing their own knowledge to bear on new learning; by anticipating learning difficulties and apportioning their time accordingly; and by judging their progress toward a learning goal. Learning environments should be designed to model and encourage the regular use of self-management strategies.

Learning as Apprenticeship

Learning environments can be organized so that complex thinking is modeled and analyzed in apprenticeship arrangements. Mentoring and coaching will enable students to undertake extended projects and develop presentations of finished work, both in and beyond the classroom.

Bibliography

Berends, Mark, Bodilly, Susan J., and Sheila N. Kirby, *Facing the Challenges of Whole-School Reform: New American Schools After a Decade*, Santa Monica, Calif.: RAND Corporation, MR-1498-EDU, 2002.

Bernhardt, V. L., "No Schools Left Behind," *Educational Leadership,* Vol. 60, No. 5, 2003, pp. 26–30.

Blase, J., and J. Blase, "Principals' Instructional Leadership and Teacher Development: Teachers' Perspectives," *Educational Administration Quarterly,* Vol. 35, No. 3, 1999, pp. 349–378.

Bodilly, Susan J., "Philanthropic Efforts at Creating Instructional Reform Through Intermediaries," paper presented at the Annual Meeting of the American Educational Research Association, Seattle, Wash., April 2001.

Bodilly, Susan J., et al., *Lessons From New American Schools' Scale-Up Phase: Prospects for Bringing Designs to Multiple Sites*, Santa Monica, Calif.: RAND Corporation, MR-942-NAS, 1998.

Boston Plan for Excellence, Introduction to CCL: Collaborative Coaching and Learning, http://www.bpe.org/pubs/CCL/Getting%20Started%20CCL.pdf, 2002, accessed September 23, 2005.

Bransford, J. D., A. L. Brown, and R. R. Cocking, eds., *How People Learn: Brain, Mind, Experience, and School*, Washington, D.C.: National Academy Press, 1999.

Bryk, A. S., and B. Schneider, *Trust in Schools: A Core Resource for Improvement*, New York: Russell Sage Foundation, 2002.

Buchen, I. H., "Overcoming Obstacles to Instructional Leadership," *Principal,* Vol. 81, No. 5, 2002, pp. 42–45.

Burch, P., and J. Spillane, *Leading from the Middle: Mid-Level District Staff and Instructional Improvement,* Chicago, Ill.: Cross City Campaign for Urban School Reform, 2004.

Choppin, J., "Data Use in Practice: Examples from the School Level," paper presented at the Annual Conference of the American Educational Research Association, New Orleans, La., April 2002.

Cohen, D. K., "What Is the System in Systemic Reform?" *Educational Researcher,* Vol. 24, No. 9, 1995, pp. 11–17.

Corcoran, T., *The Merck Institute for Science Education: A Successful Intermediary for Education Reform,* Philadelphia: Consortium for Policy Research in Education, University of Pennsylvania, CPRE Research Report Series RR-052, 2003.

Corcoran, T., and N. Lawrence, *Changing District Culture and Capacity: The Impact of the Merck Institute for Science Education Partnership,* Philadelphia: Consortium for Policy Research in Education, University of Pennsylvania, CPRE Research Report Series RR-054, 2003.

Corcoran, T., S. H. Fuhrman, and C. L. Belcher, "The District Role in Instructional Improvement," *Phi Delta Kappan,* Vol. 83, No. 1, 2001, pp. 78–84.

Council of the Great City Schools (CGCS), *Ten-Year Trends in Urban Education: 1987–1997,* Washington, D.C., March 2000.

———, "Urban School Superintendents: Characteristics, Tenure, and Salary," *Urban Indicator,* Vol. 7, No. 1, Washington, D.C., 2003.

———, *Beating the Odds: A City-by-City Analysis of Student Performance and Achievement Gaps on State Assessment Results for the 2002–2003 School Year,* Washington, D.C., 2004.

David, J. L., "Restructuring in Progress: Lessons from Pioneering Districts," in R. F. Elmore and Associates, eds., *Restructuring Schools: The Next Generation of Education Reform,* San Francisco: Jossey-Bass, 1990, pp. 209–250.

Darling-Hammond, L., "Policy for Restructuring," in A. Lieberman, ed., *The Work of Restructuring Schools: Building from the Ground Up,* New York: Teachers College Press, 1995, pp. 157–175.

———, *The Right to Learn: A Blueprint for Creating Schools that Work.* San Francisco: Jossey Bass, 1997.

Educational Research Service, *Professional Development for School Principals*, Arlington, Va.: The Informed Educator Series WS-0350, 1999.

Elmore, R. F., and D. Burney, "Investing in Teacher Learning: Staff Development and Instructional Improvement," in L. Darling-Hammond and G. Sykes, eds., *Teaching As the Learning Profession: Handbook of Policy and Practice*, San Francisco: Jossey-Bass, 1999, pp. 263–291.

Feldman, J., and R. Tung, "Whole School Reform: How Schools Use the Data-Based Inquiry and Decision Making Process," paper presented at the 82nd Annual Meeting of the American Educational Research Association, Seattle, Wash., April 2001.

Firestone, W. A., "Using Reform: Conceptualizing District Initiative," *Educational Evaluation and Policy Analysis*, Vol. 11, Summer 1989, pp. 151–164.

Fuhrman, S. H., and R. F. Elmore, "Understanding Local Control in the Wake of State Education Reform," *Educational Evaluation and Policy Analysis*, Vol. 12, No. 1, 1990, pp. 82–96.

Fullan, M., "The Return of Large-Scale Reform," *Journal of Educational Change*, Vol. 1, 2000, pp. 5–28.

Gates, S., K. Ross, and D. Brewer, *School Leadership in the Twenty-First Century: Why and How It Is Important*, Oak Brook, Ill.: North Central Regional Educational Laboratory, 2000.

George Washington University (GWU), School of Education and Human Development, Departments of Research, Teacher Preparation and Special Education, and Educational Leadership, *Montgomery County Public Schools Staff Development Teacher Program: Final Report*. Washington, D.C., 2001.

Goldring, E. B., and P. Hallinger, "District Control Contexts and School Organizational Processes," paper presented at the Annual Meeting of the American Educational Research Association, San Francisco, Calif., 1992.

Greeno, J. G., A. M. Collins, and L. B. Resnick, "Cognition and Learning," in D. C. Berliner and R. Chalfree, eds., *Handbook of Educational Psychology*, New York: Simon & Schuster, 1996, pp. 15–46.

Herman, J., and B. Gribbons, *Lessons Learned in Using Data to Support School Inquiry and Continuous Improvement: Final Report to the Stuart*

Foundation, Los Angeles, CA: National Center for Research on Evaluation, Standards, and Student Testing, 2001.

Hess, A. G., *Restructuring Urban Schools: A Chicago Perspective*, New York: Teachers College, 1995.

Hightower, A. M., M. S. Knapp, J. A. Marsh, and M. W. McLaughlin, *School Districts and Instructional Renewal*, New York: Teachers College Press, 2002.

Honig, M. I., "The New Middle Management: Intermediary Organizations in Education Policy Implementation," *Educational Evaluation and Policy Analysis*, Vol. 26, No. 1, 2004, pp. 65–87.

Honig, M. I., ed., *Confronting Complexity: Defining the Field of Education Policy Implementation*, Albany, N.Y.: SUNY Press, forthcoming.

Ingersoll, R. M., "Teacher Turnover and Teacher Shortages: An Organizational Analysis," *American Educational Research Journal*, Vol. 38, No. 3, 2001, pp. 499–534.

———, "The Teacher Shortage: Myth or Reality?" *Educational Horizons*, Vol. 81, No. 3, 2003, pp. 146–152.

Ingram, D., K. S. Louis, and R. G. Schroeder, "Accountability Policies and Teacher Decision Making: Barriers to the Use of Data to Improve Practice," *Teachers College Record*, Vol. 106, No. 6, 2004, pp. 1258–1287.

Institute for Learning, *LearningWalk^{SM} Sourcebook*, Pittsburgh, Penn.: University of Pittsburgh, 2003.

Kronley, R. A., and C. Handley, "Reforming Relationships: School Districts, External Organizations, and Systemic Change," report prepared for *School Communities That Work: A National Task Force on the Future of Urban Districts*, Providence, R.I.: Annenberg Institute for School Reform at Brown University, 2003.

Marsh, J. A., "How Districts Relate to States, Schools, and Communities: A Review of Emerging Literature," in A. M. Hightower, M. S. Knapp, J. A. Marsh, and M. W. McLaughlin, eds., *School Districts and Instructional Renewal*, New York: Teachers College Press, 2002, pp. 25–40.

Martinez, M., and J. Harvey, "From Whole School to Whole System Reform," report of a working conference sponsored by the National Clearinghouse for Comprehensive School Reform (NCCSR) in partnership with the Annenberg Institute for School Reform, the Consortium for

Policy Research in Education, and New American Schools, Washington, D.C., 2004.

Mason, S., *Turning Data Into Knowledge: Lessons from Six Milwaukee Public Schools,* Madison, Wisc.: Wisconsin Center for Education Research, 2002.

Massell, D., *The District Role in Building Capacity: Four Strategies,* Philadelphia: Consortium for Policy Research in Education, University of Pennsylvania, CPRE Policy Brief No. RB-32, 2000.

Massell, D., and M. Goertz, "Local Strategies for Building Capacity: The District Role in Supporting Instructional Reform," paper presented at the Annual Meeting of the American Educational Research Association, Montreal, Canada, 1999.

Mayer, R. E., and M. C. Wittrock, "Problem-Solving Transfer," in D. C. Berliner and R. Chalfree, eds., *Handbook of Educational Psychology,* New York: Simon & Schuster, 1996, pp. 47–62.

McLaughlin, M. W., "The RAND Change Agent Study Revisited: Macro Perspectives and Micro Realities," *Educational Researcher,* Vol. 19, 1991, pp. 11–16.

———, "How District Communities Do and Do Not Foster Teacher Pride," *Education Leadership,* Vol. 50, 1992 pp. 33–35.

McLaughlin, M. W., and D. Mitra, "Theory-Based Change and Change-Based Theory: Going Deeper, Going Broader," *Journal of Educational Change,* Vol. 2, 2001, pp. 301–323.

McLaughlin, M. W. and J. E. Talbert, *Contexts that Matter for Teaching and Learning,* Stanford, Calif.: Center for Research on the Context of Secondary School Teaching, 1993.

———, "Reforming Districts," in A. M. Hightower, M. S. Knapp, J. A. Marsh, and M. W. McLaughlin, eds., *School Districts and Instructional Renewal,* New York: Teachers College Press, 2002, pp. 173–192.

———, "Bay Area School Reform Collaborative: System Change Through Coaching and Collaboration," paper presented at Annual Meeting of the American Educational Research Association, San Diego, Calif., 2004.

MDRC, Big-City School Districts Face a Big Job, MDRC Fast Fact Archive, Washington, D.C., http://www.mdrc.org/area_fact_9.html, 2003, accessed September 23, 2005.

Murphy, J., and P. Hallinger, "The Superintendent as Instructional Leader: Findings from Effective School Districts," *The Journal of Educational Administration*, Vol. 24, No. 2, 1986, pp. 213–231.

———, "Characteristics of Instructionally Effective School Districts," *Journal of Educational Research*, Vol. 81, 1988, pp. 175–181.

National Center for Education Statistics, "Characteristics of the 100 Largest Public Elementary and Secondary School Districts in the United States: 2001–02," prepared for the Common Core of Data, Washington D.C., 2003.

National Staff Development Council, http://www.nsdc.org/library/leaders/leader_report.cfm, 2001, accessed September 23, 2005.

Neufeld, B., and D. Roper, *Growing Instructional Capacity in Two San Diego Middle Schools*, Cambridge, Mass.: Education Matters, 2003a.

———, *Coaching: A Strategy for Developing Instructional Capacity*, Providence, R.I. and Washington, D.C.: The Annenberg Institute for School Reform and The Aspen Institute Program on Education, 2003b.

Newmann, F. M., "Reducing Student Alienation in High School: Implications of Theory," *Harvard Educational Review*, Vol. 51, No. 4, 1981, pp. 546–564.

Odden, A. R., ed., *Education Policy Implementation*, Albany, N.Y.: SUNY Press, 1991.

Pittman, T. S., "Motivation," in D. T. Gilbert, S. T. Fiske, and G. Lindsay, eds., *The Handbook of Social Psychology*, Vol. 1 (4th ed.), New York: McGraw Hill, 1998, pp. 549–590.

Poglinco, S. M., A. J. Bach, K. Hovde, S. Rosenblum, M. Saunders, and J. A. Supovitz, *The Heart of the Matter: The Coaching Model in America's Choice Schools*, Philadelphia: Consortium for Policy Research in Education, University of Pennsylvania, 2003.

"Quality Counts '98: The Urban Challenge" [series], *Education Week*, 1998.

Resnick, L. B., "From Aptitude to Effort: A New Foundation for Our Schools," *Daedalus*, Vol. 124, 1995, pp. 55–62.

Resnick, L. B., and T. K. Glennan, "Leadership for Learning: A Theory of Action for Urban School Districts," in A. M. Hightower, M. S. Knapp,

J. A. Marsh, and M. W. McLaughlin, eds., *School Districts and Instructional Renewal*, New York: Teachers College Press, 2002.

Resnick, L. B., and M. W. Hall, "Learning Organizations for Sustainable Education Reform," *Journal of the American Academy of Arts and Sciences*, Vol. 127, No. 4, 1998, pp. 89–118.

Richard, A., *"Making Our Own Road": The Emergence of School-Based Staff Developers in America's Public Schools*, New York: Edna McConnell Clark Foundation, 2003.

Rosenholtz, S. J., *Teachers' Workplace: The Social Organization of School*, White Plains, N.Y.: Longman Inc., 1989.

Rothman, R., "'Intermediary Organizations' Help Bring Reform to Scale," *Challenge Journal: The Journal of the Annenberg Challenge,* Vol. 6, No. 2, 2003, pp. 1–8.

Sizer, T. R., *Horace's School: Redesigning the American High School*, New York: Houghton Mifflin, 1992.

Snipes, J., F. Doolittle, and C. Herlihy, *Foundations for Success: Case Studies of How Urban Schools Improve Student Achievement*, New York: MDRC, 2002.

Spillane, J. P., "School Districts Matter: Local Educational Authorities and State Instructional Policy," *Educational Policy*, Vol. 1, No. 1, 1996, pp. 63–87.

———, "A Cognitive Perspective on the LEA's Roles in Implementing Instructional Policy," *Education*, Evanston, Ill.: Northwestern University, 20, 1997.

———, "State Policy and the Non-Monolithic Nature of the Local School District: Organizational and Professional Considerations," *American Educational Research Journal*, Vol. 35, No. 1, 1998, pp. 33–63.

———, *Standards Deviation: How Schools Misunderstand Education Policy,* Cambridge, Mass.: Harvard University Press, 2004.

Spillane, J. P., and C. L. Thompson, "Reconstructing Conceptions of Local Capacity: The Local Educational Agency's Capacity for Ambitious Instructional Reform," *Education Evaluation and Policy Analysis*, Vol. 19, No. 2, 1997, pp. 185–203.

Spillane, J. P., R. Halverson, and J. Diamond, "Distributed Leadership: Toward a Theory of School Leadership Practice," paper presented at the

Annual Meeting of the American Educational Research Association, Montreal, Canada, 1999.

———, "Investigating School Leadership Practice: A Distributed Perspective," *Education Researcher*, Vol. 30, 2001, pp. 23–28.

Staub, F. C., and D. D. Bickel, "Developing Content-Focused Coaching in Elementary Literacy: A Case Study on Designing for Scale," paper presented at European Association for Research on Learning and Instruction, Padova, Italy, August 2003.

Supovitz, J. A., and V. Klein, Mapping a Course for Improved Student Learning: How Innovative Schools Systematically Use Student Performance Data to Guide Improvement, Philadelphia, Penn.: Consortium for Policy Research in Education, University of Pennsylvania, 2003.

Togneri, W., and S. E. Anderson, *Beyond Islands of Excellence: What Districts Can Do to Improve Instruction and Achievement in All Schools*, Washington D.C.: Learning First Alliance, 2003.

Vargo, M., "Choices and Consequences in the Bay Area School Reform Collaborative: Building the Capacity to Scale Up Whole-School Improvement," in T. K. Glennan, Jr., S. J. Bodilly, J. R. Galegher, and K. A. Kerr, eds., *Expanding the Reach of Education Reforms: Perspectives from Leaders in the Scale-Up of Educational Interventions*, Santa Monica, Calif.: RAND Corporation, MG-248-FF, 2004, pp. 565–602.

Vargo, M., and N. Toussaint, "Walter Annenberg's Dream," *Education Week*, November 6, 2002, Vol. 22, No. 10, pp. 38, 52.

West, L., and F. C. Staub, "Content-Focused Coaching[SM]: Transforming Mathematics Lessons," Portsmouth, New Hampshire: Heinemann, 2003.